CW00500972

THE UNOFFICIAL HALLOWEEN COOKBOOK FOR HARRY POTTER FANS

THE UNOFFICIAL HALLOWEEN COOKBOOK FOR HARRY POTTER FANS

Inspired Recipes *for the* Spookiest *of* Holidays

Written by Tom Grimm

Photography by Tom Grimm & Dimitrie Harder
Translated by Andy Jones Berasaluce

Skyhorse Publishing

Skyhorse Publishing books may be purchased in bulk at special discounts for sales promotion, corporate gifts, fund-raising, or educational purposes. Special editions can also be created to specifications. For details, contact the Special Sales Department, Skyhorse Publishing, 307 West 36th Street, 11th Floor, New York, NY 10018 or info@skyhorsepublishing.com.

Visit our website at www.skyhorsepublishing.com.

10 9 8 7 6 5 4 3 2 1

Library of Congress Cataloging-in-Publication Data is available on file.

Project Manager: Hannah Kwella
Editing & Compilation, Texts & Recipes: Tom Grimm, Grinning Cat Productions
Food Photography: Dimitrie Harder & Tom Grimm
Graphic Design, Typesetting & Layout: Roberts Urlovskis
Cover Design: Roberts Urlovskis
Cover Illustrations & Inside Illustrations: Angelos Tsirigotis

Print ISBN: 978-1-5107-7419-3
Ebook ISBN: 978-1-5107-7420-9

Printed in China

For

Michél Kevin Hubel

(1983-2020)

Keep an eye on us from up there.

Contents

Introduction

Every year on October 31st, in many places around the world, people say: "Trick or treat?" What kind of a question is that?

Trick, of course!

Anyone who knows me knows that (aside from my family) I love few things as much as the Wizarding World of Harry Potter: namely good food, bad jokes, amusement parks, the band Rammstein, holidays—and Halloween! Forget Easter, Christmas, New Year's, and World Pretzel Day—the only relevant holiday for me has always been the evening before All Saints' Day, when everything from hell emerges. Ghosts, goblins, trolls, and demons roam the earth freely and undisturbed, pulling practical jokes on the unsuspecting little humans who think all these creatures of darkness are merely disguised as werewolves, vampires, zombies, and ghouls.

Naturally, unsuspecting only applies to the Muggles among us who are blind to all the magic and wonder our world holds in store for those willing to take a closer look. Like the spellcasters and Potterheads out there! Thanks in no small part to the Harry Potter series, we know the meaning of Halloween.

Deaths of beloved family members, battles with trolls, the opening of secret chambers, magic school competitions . . . quite a bit happens on Halloween. And, if you remember, since Sir Nicholas de Mimsy-Porpington has haunted Hogwarts as Nearly Headless Nick, throwing a small celebration every year to commemorate his Death Day, to which Harry, Ron, and Hermione are also invited during their first year at the School of Witchcraft and Wizardry. Even if it is an honor for the friends to attend, they would've preferred to do so without seeing their host's rather questionable choice of food.

And speaking of questionable food choices!

I've got some offerings that I'm sure Sir Nicholas would be delighted with!

Ready for a puke test?

How about some horror'd'oeuvres with Demon Fingers, Stuffed Cockroaches, Grub Worms, or Eyeball Punch? Or I can highly recommend the Crazy-Eyed Skewers, Bat Blood Soup, Sneaky Sandwich, Dragon Meatballs, Spoiled Fish, and the Bacon-Wrapped Tarantula Eyes. And to make the next visit to Madam Pomfrey in the Hospital Wing worthwhile, there's such magnificent tastelessness afterward, such as Chopped Toffees, Moldy Peanuts, the Worst Jelly Beans in the World, Gravestone Cakes with Tar Glaze, and the Monster of a Tome, washed down with a hearty gulp of Restoration Potion or Swamp Juice. All lovingly prepared, of course, since you eat (with) your eyes first!

On that note: Bon appétit!

Sincerely,

Tom Grimm

RIP
RIP

Demon Fingers

Since not everyone has notable cooking skills or can fall back on magic, individual recipes in this book are kept so simple that even a troll could prepare them. This applies, for example, to this dish, which can be made very easily.

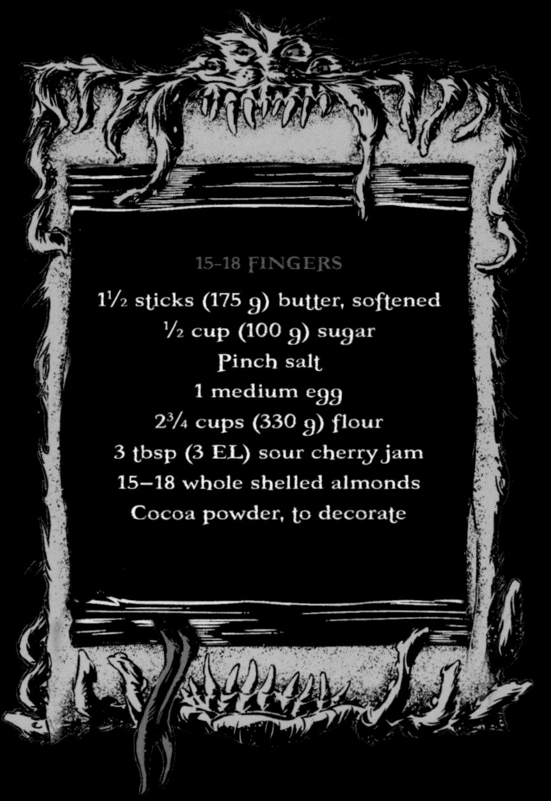

15–18 FINGERS

1½ sticks (175 g) butter, softened
½ cup (100 g) sugar
Pinch salt
1 medium egg
2¾ cups (330 g) flour
3 tbsp (3 EL) sour cherry jam
15–18 whole shelled almonds
Cocoa powder, to decorate

1. Preheat the oven to 355°F (180°C), and line a baking sheet with parchment paper.
2. In a bowl, beat the butter, sugar, and salt with a hand mixer, then add the egg. Mix thoroughly. Add the flour, and knead well using the mixer's dough hook. Wrap the dough tightly in plastic wrap and let it rest in the refrigerator for at least 30 minutes.
3. Unwrap the dough from the plastic. On a lightly floured work surface, shape the dough with your hands into long, thin cylinders about 6 inches (15 cm) long. Apply some pressure in the appropriate places so that the knuckles of the Dementor's fingers remain a bit thicker than the rest (see image). Place the dough fingers on the prepared baking sheet, spaced slightly apart.
4. Slightly round off one end of each dough finger and lightly press it in to form the fingertip. Put a small dollop of jam on top. Place an almond on top as a fingernail and press gently. Using a small, sharp knife, score two to three evenly spaced parallel grooves into the knuckles.
5. Place the baking sheet in the oven for about 15 to 20 minutes, or until the demon fingers start to brown. Then remove and let fully cool on the sheet.
6. For the finishing touch, use a small pastry brush to apply some cocoa powder around the fingernails and the knuckle folds. Dip the chopped-off end of each finger in the sour cherry jam and let dry for a few minutes.

Swamp Juice

Muddy, black swamps aren't easy to escape. In a way, the same is true of this swill made of cola, vodka, coffee, and orange liqueurs. Sound terrible? It is! Terribly tasty!

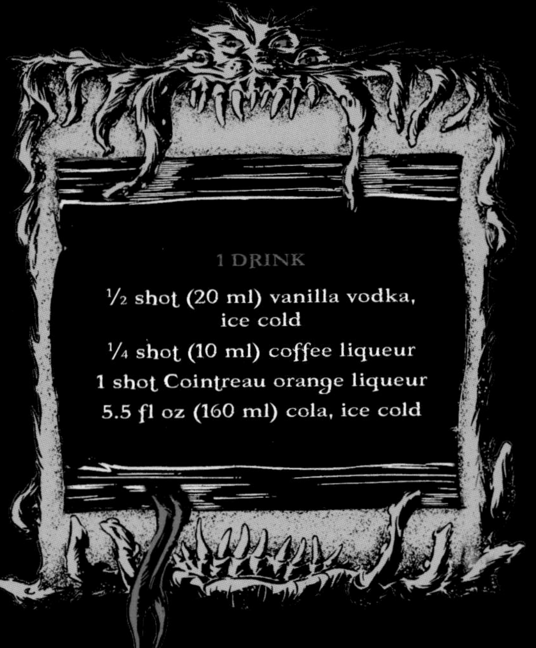

1 DRINK

½ shot (20 ml) vanilla vodka, ice cold

¼ shot (10 ml) coffee liqueur

1 shot Cointreau orange liqueur

5.5 fl oz (160 ml) cola, ice cold

1. Pour the vodka, coffee liqueur, and Cointreau into a glass. Pour in the cola, stir briefly, and serve immediately!

Bones & Skeleton

After the worms have had their fun with the dearly departed, the graveyard's culinary delights have hardly run out! Ghouls especially, fed up with subsisting on spiders and moths in witches' and wizards' attics, regularly make trips to the nearest cemetery to find something to nibble on, preferably bones and skeletons. While it might not be for everyone, as we all know, there's no accounting for taste.

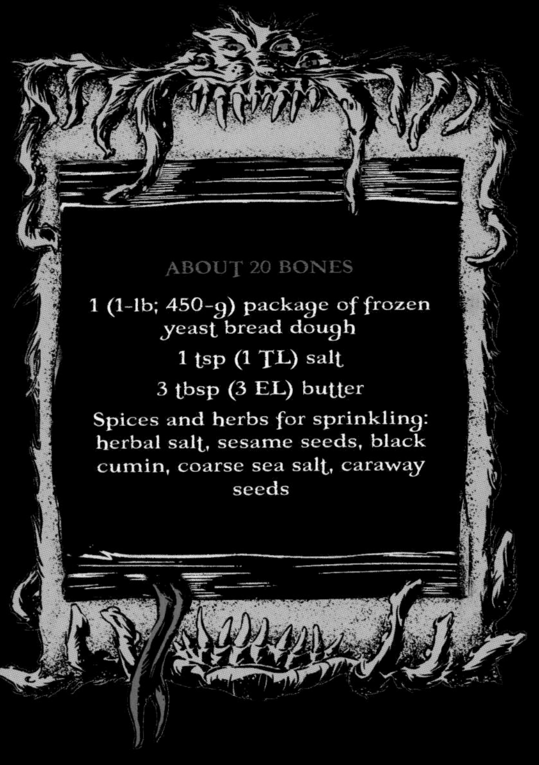

ABOUT 20 BONES

1 (1-lb; 450-g) package of frozen yeast bread dough

1 tsp (1 TL) salt

3 tbsp (3 EL) butter

Spices and herbs for sprinkling: herbal salt, sesame seeds, black cumin, coarse sea salt, caraway seeds

1. Thaw the frozen yeast dough according to the package instructions. Then knead well with your hands and leave the dough covered in a warm place for about 1 hour.
2. Add the salt to the dough and knead it well again. Then, using a rolling pin, roll the dough out on a lightly floured, smooth work surface and shape into a rectangle. Cut, using a small, sharp knife, into strips 4 inches (10 cm) long and ¾ inches (2 cm) wide. Knead the excess dough again and follow the prior process until all the dough is used up.
3. Round the edges of the dough strips by gently rolling them into a dough sausage with your hands, so the bones are narrower in the middle and thicker toward the ends (see image). Place the bones slightly apart on a baking sheet lined with parchment paper.
4. Melt the butter in the microwave and brush the bones with it. Now sprinkle the spices and herbs on top. Then let rest for another 20 to 30 minutes.
5. Meanwhile, preheat the oven to 355°F (180°C).
6. Finally, bake the bones until golden and crispy (about 15–20 minutes). Remove and let slightly cool on the sheet before serving.

POTION

Moldy Peanuts

These peanuts may be a few decades past their expiration date, but I'm sure everyone will be racing to try this delicacy—then racing to the nearest lavatory!

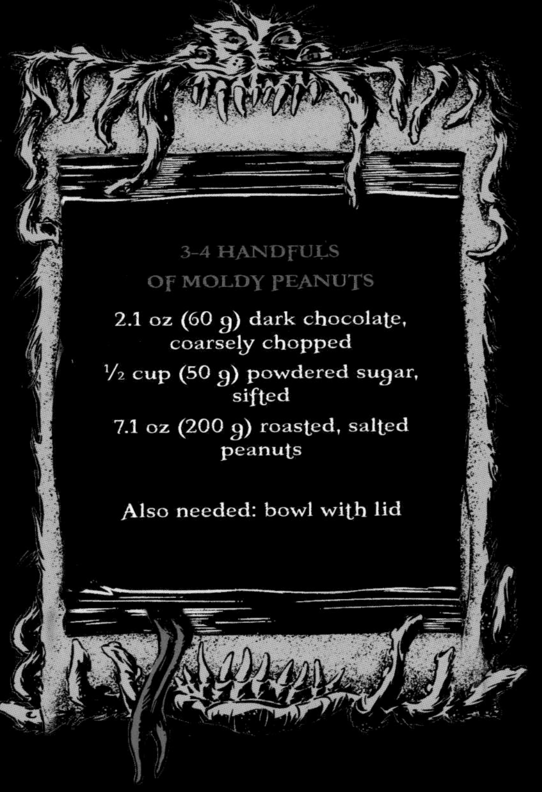

3-4 HANDFULS OF MOLDY PEANUTS

2.1 oz (60 g) dark chocolate, coarsely chopped

½ cup (50 g) powdered sugar, sifted

7.1 oz (200 g) roasted, salted peanuts

Also needed: bowl with lid

1. Melt the coarsely chopped chocolate using a bain-marie. Make sure the bottom of the bowl doesn't touch the boiling water!
2. Place the powdered sugar in a bowl with a lid.
3. Remove the bowl of melted chocolate from the heat. Add the peanuts and mix thoroughly so they are fully coated with chocolate. Then pour the peanuts into the bowl of powdered sugar, close the lid, and shake vigorously for 1 minute or until the peanuts are completely coated.
4. Open the bowl, place the peanuts on a baking sheet lined with parchment paper, and let them dry while making sure the nuts do not stick together.
5. Once the peanuts have dried, put them in a coarse sieve to gently shake off any excess powdered sugar. Store in an airtight sealable container.

Slime Soup

A very special horror awaits your palate with this soup! It's very easy to prepare: just toss whatever the back of your pantry has to offer into a large pot, add a few cups of water, simmer on low for a few days until even the toughest gristles become buttery soft, and serve with some Raven-Charred Pastries (p. 51) and Pull-Apart Magical Bubble Bread (p. 83). Sounds delicious, doesn't it? (Yeah, not delicious sounding!)

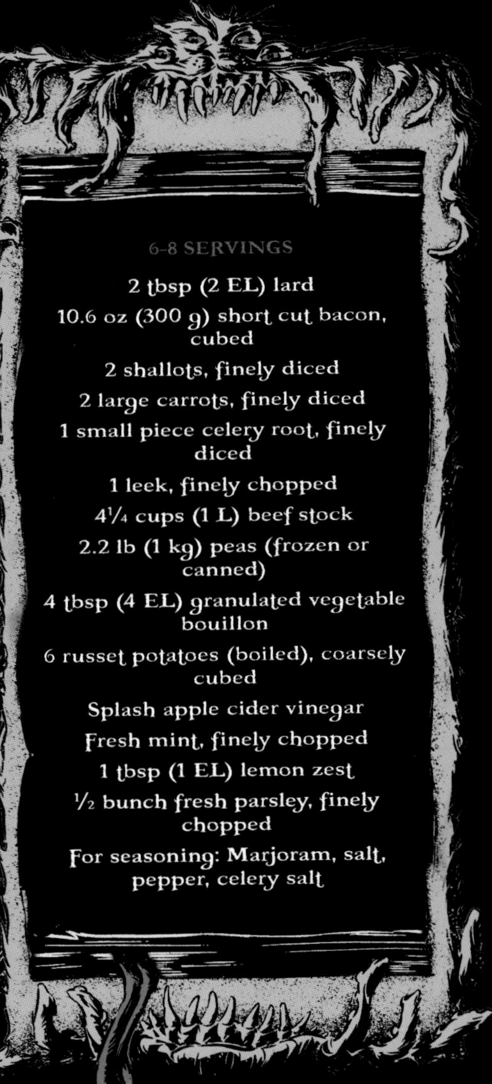

6–8 SERVINGS

2 tbsp (2 EL) lard
10.6 oz (300 g) short cut bacon, cubed
2 shallots, finely diced
2 large carrots, finely diced
1 small piece celery root, finely diced
1 leek, finely chopped
4¼ cups (1 L) beef stock
2.2 lb (1 kg) peas (frozen or canned)
4 tbsp (4 EL) granulated vegetable bouillon
6 russet potatoes (boiled), coarsely cubed
Splash apple cider vinegar
Fresh mint, finely chopped
1 tbsp (1 EL) lemon zest
½ bunch fresh parsley, finely chopped
For seasoning: Marjoram, salt, pepper, celery salt

1. In a large pot, melt the lard over medium-high heat. Fry the bacon cubes in it for 1 to 2 minutes, until crisp. Add the shallots and sauté until translucent. Then add the diced carrots, celery root, and leek, mix well, and cook for 5 minutes, stirring regularly. Deglaze with the beef stock and bring everything to a gentle simmer.
2. Add the peas, vegetable bouillon, and a good pinch of marjoram. Let simmer for 30 minutes on medium heat. Then add the cubed potatoes, reduce the heat to low, and simmer for an hour, stirring occasionally. Add a generous splash of apple cider vinegar, the fresh mint, and some fresh lemon zest. Finally, stir in the chopped parsley and simmer for another 5 minutes.
3. Remove from the stove and let cool a little. Then finely (but not too finely!) puree with an immersion blender. Season with salt, pepper, celery salt, lovage, and, if necessary, a little more marjoram.

Like most stews, this one tastes especially delicious the next day, when it's had time to steep and allow the flavors to really develop. It's best prepared the day before serving. Just gently warm it up again ahead of the meal!

Worm Salad

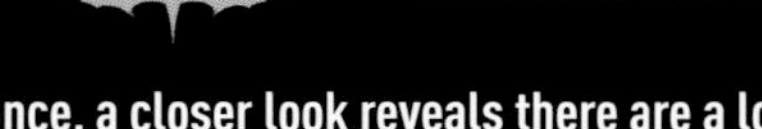

Even if it doesn't seem so at first glance, a closer look reveals there are a lot of goodies in cemeteries—at least if you enjoy delicacies like bones, grave moss, or worms. This recipe is recommended for all those adventurous souls!

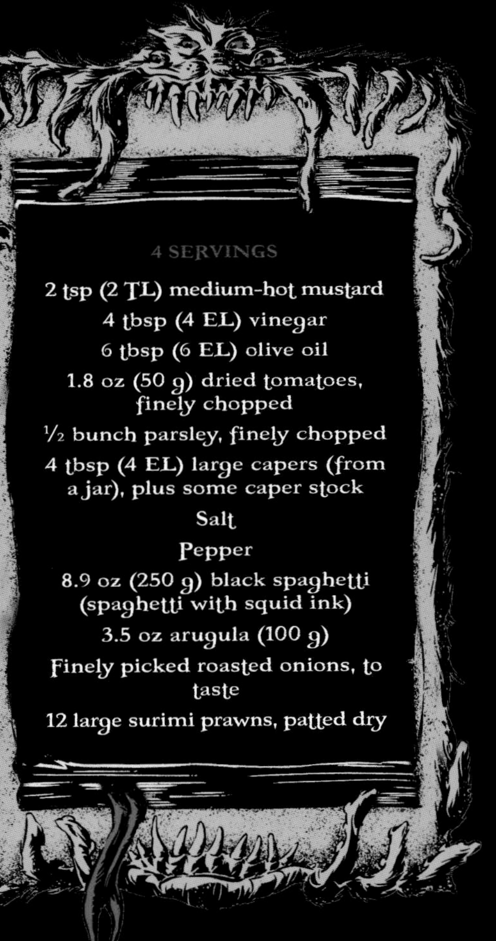

4 SERVINGS

2 tsp (2 TL) medium-hot mustard

4 tbsp (4 EL) vinegar

6 tbsp (6 EL) olive oil

1.8 oz (50 g) dried tomatoes, finely chopped

½ bunch parsley, finely chopped

4 tbsp (4 EL) large capers (from a jar), plus some caper stock

Salt

Pepper

8.9 oz (250 g) black spaghetti (spaghetti with squid ink)

3.5 oz arugula (100 g)

Finely picked roasted onions, to taste

12 large surimi prawns, patted dry

1. In a large bowl, mix the mustard with the vinegar and oil. Add the tomatoes, parsley, and capers. Add a dash of caper stock, season with salt and pepper, and gently mix everything together.
2. Follow the package instructions to cook the black spaghetti. Drain the noodles well using a colander and collect the cooking water as you drain. Then return the spaghetti to the pot and mix with 2 tablespoons (2 EL) of the cooking water.
3. Add the spaghetti to the bowl with the vinaigrette. Fold in the arugula and roasted onions. Gently mix everything together. Arrange on deep plates, place three surimi prawns on top of each dish, and serve immediately.

If you don't have any squid ink on hand, you can simply color normal pasta with black food coloring after cooking and draining. Don't overdo it with the salt! The capers, arugula, and horseradish already provide enough seasoning!

Giant Spider Goo

Basic rule: Eating spider eggs is strongly discouraged as it can be detrimental to your health! Not so much the eggs themselves, rather trying to get ahold of them, because giant spiders are very reluctant to give up their offspring.

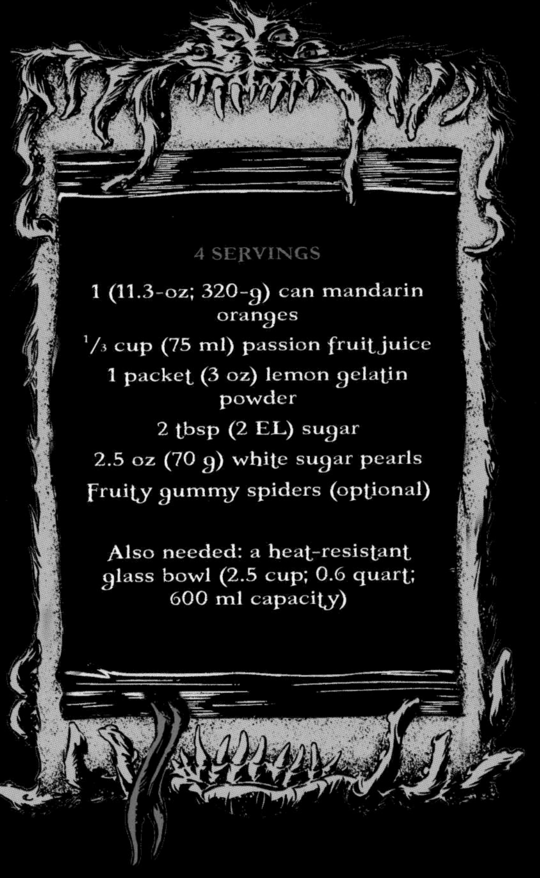

4 SERVINGS

1 (11.3-oz; 320-g) can mandarin oranges

1/3 cup (75 ml) passion fruit juice

1 packet (3 oz) lemon gelatin powder

2 tbsp (2 EL) sugar

2.5 oz (70 g) white sugar pearls

Fruity gummy spiders (optional)

Also needed: a heat-resistant glass bowl (2.5 cup; 0.6 quart; 600 ml capacity)

1. Chill the glass bowl in the refrigerator.
2. Drain the mandarin oranges using a sieve. Collect the juice and put it in a beaker along with the passion fruit juice. Pour in up to 2 cups of water, mix, and place in a small saucepan.
3. Add the gelatin powder and sugar to the saucepan and heat over medium heat, stirring constantly, until the sugar has completely dissolved. Remove from the stove and let cool.
4. Place the sugar pearls in the chilled bowl and pour in some of the gelatin dessert. Stir with a spoon until all the pearls are covered with liquid. Then spread the pearls with a spoon so that they form a thin, closed layer at the bottom of the dish. Place in the refrigerator for about 15 minutes so the gelatin sets and the pearls stick to it.
5. Now add just over half the remaining gelatin dessert and the mandarins. Put the bowl back in the refrigerator until the gelatin has set slightly. Then add the remaining liquid and refrigerate preferably overnight, but for at least 6 hours, until the gelatin has set completely.
6. Using a sharp knife, carefully loosen the gelatin from the bowl's edges and gently flip onto a large, flat serving plate. Decorate as you like with fruity gummy spiders. Serve immediately

World's Worst Jelly Beans

Ah, a culinary classic, even though not every flavor is necessarily delicious! Think of such questionable varieties as dog food, dirty socks, and boogers. With this recipe, you can make your own beans. How gross they are is up to you!

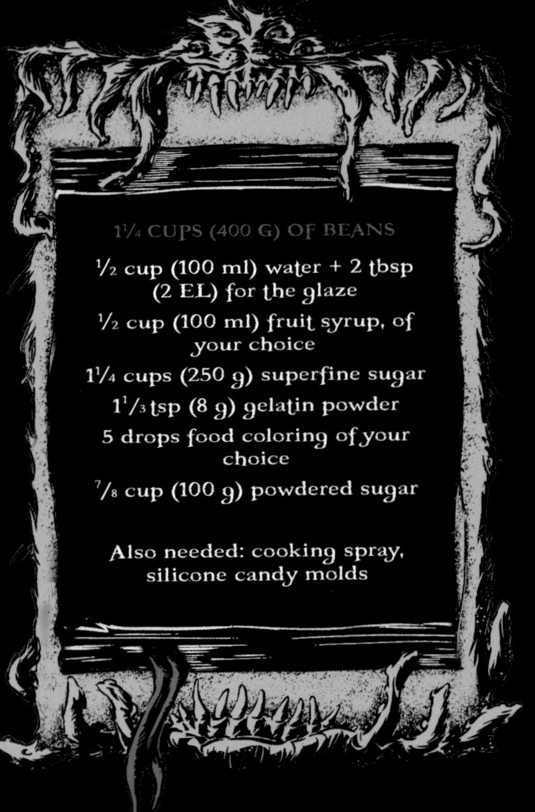

1¼ CUPS (400 G) OF BEANS

½ cup (100 ml) water + 2 tbsp (2 EL) for the glaze

½ cup (100 ml) fruit syrup, of your choice

1¼ cups (250 g) superfine sugar

1⅓ tsp (8 g) gelatin powder

5 drops food coloring of your choice

⅞ cup (100 g) powdered sugar

Also needed: cooking spray, silicone candy molds

1. Pour ½ cup (100 ml) water, the fruit syrup, and the sugar into a saucepan. Heat over low heat, stirring constantly and gently, until the sugar has completely dissolved. Then stir the gelatin powder into the sugar syrup.
2. Heat, stirring constantly, until the syrup reaches 230°F (110°C) (about 20 minutes). Be extremely careful when doing this, as the syrup is very hot. If it splashes the skin, it can cause severe burns! Regularly check the temperature with a candy thermometer.
3. Spray the silicone molds liberally with cooking spray.
4. As soon as the syrup has reached the required temperature, stir in your chosen food coloring and pour the sugar syrup evenly into the silicone molds. Smooth off with a spatula. Wrap the molds in plastic wrap and let settle overnight.
5. In a small bowl, mix the powdered sugar with 2 tablespoons (2 EL) of water until smooth. Carefully remove the bean halves from the molds. Brush the top surface of each bean half with the glaze, then stick them together and let dry for 30 minutes. Store in an airtight sealable container.

Using this recipe, you can make beans in any flavor you want—even gross ones! All you have to do is add 1 tablespoon (1 EL) of savory ingredients like onion or garlic powder!

Bat Bites

A lot of people hate bats—which I think can only be because they don't know how delicious bats taste! They're a wicked treat for the palate, especially when prepared as they are here. Seriously: these fluttering critters are lucky to be a protected species, otherwise they'd probably have been eaten up . . . err, extinct by now!

16 BAT BITES

17.6 oz (500 g) firm cream cheese

Coarse black pepper

16 green or black olives with pimento

Bag of tortilla chips (darkest color possible)

1. Using your hands, form 16 bite-size balls of cream cheese.
2. Place the coarse black pepper in a small bowl and roll the cream cheese balls around in it to coat them in pepper. Place the balls slightly apart on a plate, cover loosely with plastic wrap, and refrigerate for 1 hour to set.
3. Halve the pimento-stuffed olives and place them upside down (with the cut part on top) as eyes on the cream cheese balls.
4. Stick the square tortilla chips into the sides of the cream cheese balls as wings. Using a sharp knife, carefully cut off the corners of a few chips and place them on the balls as ears.
5. Store in the refrigerator until ready to serve.

A Monster of a Tome

Some magical books are known to run away, hide, bite, and snap their covers to avoid being opened and flipped through. This version of the work, on the other hand, is far more pleasant, and can't wait for you to check out what's inside! And believe me: it's quite a bit!

1 CAKE

For the cake:

2 sticks + 1½ tbsp (250 g) softened butter
¾ cup (150 g) sugar
1 packet (0.32 oz) vanilla sugar
Pinch salt
3 medium eggs
1 cup (150 g) flour
2 tsp (2 TL) baking powder
1 heaping tbsp (1 EL) cocoa powder
2 tbsp (2 EL) milk
5.3 oz (150 g) milk chocolate, finely chopped

For the filling:

3 sticks (330 g) soft butter
1 packet (0.32 oz) vanilla sugar
5¼ cups (600 g) powdered sugar
½ cup (120 ml) milk

For the buttercream:

2 sticks +1½ tbsp (330 g) softened butter
¾ cup (90 g) cocoa powder
5¼ cups (600 g) powdered sugar
½ cup (120 ml) milk

To decorate:

Red fondant (for the bookmark), orange fondant (for the eyes), white fondant (for the teeth), black food coloring pen (for the eyes)

Also needed: icing/piping bag, piping nozzles, rectangular baking pan (16 × 11 × 4 inches; 40 × 30 × 10 cm)

Cake preparation:

1. Preheat the oven to 355°F (180°C). Grease the baking pan with butter.
2. In a mixing bowl, using a hand mixer, blend the butter, sugar, vanilla sugar, and salt until creamy. Gradually add the eggs one by one. Mix well. Through a sieve, add the flour, baking powder, and cocoa powder, and mix these in. Lastly add the milk and finely chopped chocolate. Mix on low for 1 minute. Then pour the batter into the buttered pan, smooth off the top, and bake for about 45 minutes. Remove and let cool completely in the mold. In the meantime, prepare the filling and buttercream.

Vanilla filling and the chocolate buttercream:

3. For the filling, mix the butter and the vanilla sugar in a mixing bowl using a hand mixer. Gradually add the powdered sugar, mixing thoroughly each time. Then, pouring a little at a time, add the milk and mix until achieving desired consistency.
4. Do the same with the ingredients for the chocolate buttercream.

Put it all together:

5. Using a large knife, cut the cooled cake down the middle horizontally to create two equal halves. Place one of the halves on the work surface and evenly spread 2/3 of the vanilla filling on top. Then carefully place the other half of the cake on top and evenly spread the rest of the light cream all around. Spread with a spatula so that it resembles the pages of a book.

(Continued on next page)

6. Roll out the red fondant with a rolling pin to about ¾ inch (2 cm) thick. Use a small, sharp knife to cut out a long, thin rectangle and stick it on top of the buttercream as a bookmark (see picture).
7. Using the orange fondant, form four little balls the size of cherries and draw the eyes on with the black food coloring pen.
8. Shape the lips from the remaining red fondant and use the white fondant to make some crooked teeth.
9. Insert the chocolate buttercream in a piping bag with a fine-tipped nozzle and pipe the hairs onto the book. Apply a little more cream to the area where the eyes will go, so it raises them up on a sort or ridge from the rest of the cover. Place the eyes here, evenly spaced, and press lightly. Finally attach the mouth and teeth to the chocolate cream and let your masterpiece rest for an hour before serving.

Enchanted Hat

With this recipe, you can bring this magical hat into your home—the only house that really matters for a human like you! Don't be intimidated by the directions for this one. You can do it!

1 CAKE

For the cake base:
11 eggs
2¾ cups (550 g) sugar
2¼ cups (550 ml) milk
2¼ cups (550 ml) oil
3 packets (0.32 oz each) vanilla sugar
2 pinches salt
3½ tbsp (2½ packets) baking powder
¾ cup (80 g) cocoa powder
6 cups (750 g) flour

For the milk chocolate ganache:
1¾ cups (400 g) cream
2.2 lb (1 kg) milk chocolate, coarsely chopped

For the chocolate buttercream:
1½ packets (5.85 oz) chocolate pudding
2½ cups (600 ml) milk
3 tbsp (3 EL) sugar
3 sticks (375 g) soft butter, at room temperature
Vanilla extract, to taste
¾ cup (75 g) powdered sugar

For the chocolate crisped rice treats:
1½ tbsp (20 g) butter
7.1 oz (200 g) marshmallows
8 cups (200 g) Cocoa Krispies

For the garnish:
3.5 oz (100 g) brittle
3.5 oz (100 g) chocolate shavings
4.4 lb (2 kg) bakers' chocolate
Black and brown food coloring powder

Also needed:
Three round springform pans (6 inches, 7 inches, 8 inches; 15 cm, 18 cm, 20 cm), silicone mat, wooden sticks

Prepare the cake base:

1. Line the baking pans with parchment paper. Preheat the oven to 350°F (175°C).
2. In a bowl, using a hand mixer, beat the eggs with the sugar until very creamy. Gently stir in the milk and oil, then briefly work in the vanilla sugar, salt, baking powder, cocoa, and flour. Pour the dough evenly into the different-sized baking tins, smooth off the tops, and bake according to the size of your cake base.

   6 inch (15 cm) = 30 minutes
   7 inch (18 cm) = 40 minutes
   8 inch (20 cm) = 45 minutes

3. Remove from the oven, let cool in the molds, and then cut each layer in thirds horizontally with a large knife so that you have nine round cake bases.

Prepare the milk chocolate ganache:

4. Briefly bring the cream to a boil in a saucepan, stirring constantly. Remove from the heat and add the chopped chocolate to the cream. Leave for a few minutes until the chocolate has melted, then stir until smooth. Allow to cool to room temperature.

Prepare the chocolate buttercream:

5. Following the instructions on the package, prepare a thick pudding from the pudding powder, milk, and sugar, stirring constantly. Remove from the stove, cover with plastic wrap, and allow to cool to room temperature.
6. Place the softened butter (which must also be at room temperature!) in a bowl. Using a food processor or a hand mixer, beat together the butter, vanilla, and powdered sugar for a few minutes until very fluffy and light. Then gradually add the cooled, still easily pourable pudding and stir in until the whole thing forms a homogeneous cream.

(Continued on next page)

Prepare the chocolate crisped rice treats:

7. Put the butter and marshmallows in a nonstick pan and melt slowly over low heat. Add the Cocoa Krispies and fold them in with a well-greased, heatproof spatula. Caution: the mixture is very hot!
8. Let cool slightly so you can handle the blend without burning your fingers. Then place the compound on a silicone mat and, with greased hands, knead everything well. You can take some of the batter and squeeze it a little to make it firmer and more compact, depending on how big you want the tip of the Enchanted Hat to be. Then shape the tip of the hat out of the batter (see picture). Leave in the refrigerator to harden a bit.
9. Roll individual pieces of the remaining Krispies batter between your palms, as these will later be the eyebrows and mouth affixed to the layer cake. Here you can let your imagination run wild!

Put it all together:

10. Once everything's prepared, start stacking the cake bases. First place an 8-inch (20 cm) cake base on the work surface, then spread the buttercream evenly on it and sprinkle with brittle and chocolate shavings. Then put the next 8-inch (20 cm) base on top of the other one. Again, spread with buttercream and sprinkle with brittle and chocolate shavings. Repeat with the third 8-inch (20 cm) base. Then continue the same process with the three 7-inch (18 cm) bases, and finally, with the 6-inch (15 cm) bases, so that the cake cone gets a little narrower toward the top. Continue until all bases are stacked. Chill uncovered in the refrigerator for an hour.
11. Using a large, sharp knife, carve the hat's shape out of the cake cone, like a sculptor would from a block of stone. Trim off the excess. It's best to use the picture as a guide for this part.
12. Once finished, attach the hardened hat tip to the top of the cake with a wooden stick. Cover the hat with a layer of ganache. Using some buttercream, adhere the face to the front of the hat. Adjust and set the pieces into place with toothpicks if necessary. Refrigerate the whole cake again, at least for 3 or 4 hours, though preferably overnight.
13. Meanwhile, knead the chocolate fondant until it is smooth. Roll it out to a ¼-inch (5 mm) thickness on a work surface sprinkled with baking starch. Leave some fondant for the brim of the hat and a thin decorative band.
14. Cover the tip of the hat with fondant first, then the rest of the cake. To do so, roll, using the rolling pin, out a large fondant rectangle and place it over the hat's body so that the ends meet at the back. Join the seams, then press the fondant down all around. Cut off excess fondant with a small, sharp knife. Then make folds along the fondant for wrinkles; the Enchanted Hat is quite a few years old, after all. Run your hands over the hat's facial features several times to smooth them out.
15. Roll out a wide strip of fondant to form the hat's brim and drape it around the hat. Also form a narrow strip to really emphasize the connection between the hat body and the brim. The hat should now look essentially how it is meant to look. Last but not least, give your artwork the final touch by evenly applying the food coloring powder with a brush. Shade the front areas lighter and those further back darker. That's a wrap. All you have to do now is let your friends and family celebrate your hard work. You've earned it!

INDOR

Screaming Potted Plant Babies

Wizards and witches know of countless plants and herbs with special magical properties. One of them may bear a certain resemblance to a human baby—and is also at least as annoying as one. Great caution is a must when caring for these enchanted plants, as their screams can knock someone out. It is therefore strongly advised to wear earmuffs when cultivating this very special species. It doesn't do anything, but it sure looks appropriately dramatic!

10 POTTED PLANTS

For the muffins:

1¾ cup + 2 tbsp (300g) flour
¾ cup (80 g) cocoa powder
1 tsp (1 TL) baking powder
1 tsp (1 TL) baking soda
Pinch salt
7 tbsp (100 g) butter, softened
1 cup (220 g) sugar
1 tsp (1 TL) vanilla extract
2 eggs
1 cup + 1 tbsp (250 ml) buttermilk
5.3 oz (150 g) dark chocolate, coarsely chopped

For the plants:

14.1 oz (400 g) marzipan dough
Some cocoa powder for dusting
20 herb leaves (e.g., basil, mint)

For the chocolate frosting:

5.25 oz (150 g) cream cheese
1 tbsp + 2 tsp (15 g) powdered sugar
1 heaping tbsp (1 EL) cocoa powder

Also needed: 3 paper muffin cups, 10 small food-safe clay pots

1. Soak the clay pots in water for about an hour. Cut appropriately sized circles out of the parchment paper and place one at the bottom of each pot.
2. Preheat the oven to 390°F (200°C).
3. Mix the flour, cocoa, baking powder, baking soda, and salt in a small bowl. In a separate, larger bowl, using a hand mixer, beat the butter, sugar, and vanilla into a cream. Add the eggs one by one and beat until fluffy. Stir in the buttermilk thoroughly.
4. In the smaller bowl, fold the dry ingredients into the butter mixture. Measure out enough batter for three muffins and pour into the muffin tin. Fold the chocolate into the rest of the batter and pour into the clay pots. Place the pots and the muffin tin in the oven for about 25 minutes. Remove and let cool completely. Remove the muffins from the tin and crumble coarsely.
5. Divide the marzipan into 10 equal pieces and form rough shapes from the individual pieces. Flatten the bottom a little. Give the plants some character, using a toothpick, knife, and spoon. To do so, score small grooves across the body with a knife, press in the eyes with a toothpick, shape the mouth with a spoon, and, if desired, form little arms. Dust with cocoa. Finally, poke a hole in each head with a toothpick. Put in the refrigerator.
6. Combine the cream cheese, powdered sugar, and cocoa powder in a small bowl and stir until smooth. Spread the frosting generously on the top of the muffins in the clay pots, stick the plant babies on top and decorate all around with crumbled muffin dirt. Stick the herb leaves into the previously made holes in the head.

Giant Spider Eggs

According to a highly scientific study, all spiders in the world combined eat 800 million tons of prey annually. That means they could fill up on everyone on earth in 12 months and still be famished. And those are just the regular arachnids! If you then add in monster spiders, humanity would probably be gone by the end of the week. Given that, it seems only fair to beat them to the punch and feast on their offspring in kind!

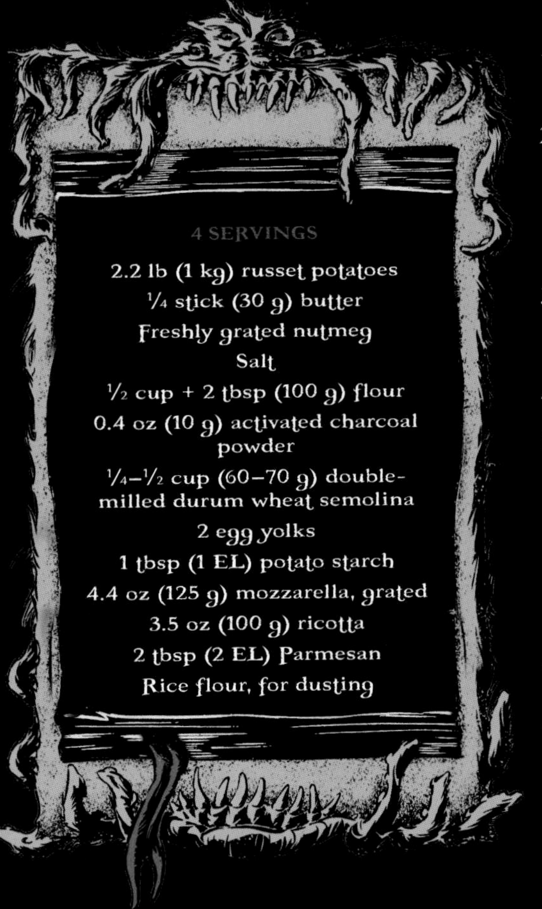

4 SERVINGS

2.2 lb (1 kg) russet potatoes
¼ stick (30 g) butter
Freshly grated nutmeg
Salt
½ cup + 2 tbsp (100 g) flour
0.4 oz (10 g) activated charcoal powder
¼–½ cup (60–70 g) double-milled durum wheat semolina
2 egg yolks
1 tbsp (1 EL) potato starch
4.4 oz (125 g) mozzarella, grated
3.5 oz (100 g) ricotta
2 tbsp (2 EL) Parmesan
Rice flour, for dusting

1. Preheat the oven, using the convection setting, to 320°F (160°C).
2. Wash and dry the unpeeled potatoes, then place on a baking sheet lined with parchment paper. Cook in the preheated oven for about an hour. Then remove and let cool until the potatoes are lukewarm. Peel, press twice through a potato ricer and let the mash cool.
3. In the meantime, melt the butter in a small saucepan over medium-high heat. Add some freshly grated nutmeg and 1 tablespoon (1 EL) salt. Mix well.
4. Mix the flour and activated charcoal in a small bowl.
5. Dust the work surface with some durum wheat semolina and sprinkle the flour and charcoal mixture over it. Add the mashed potatoes and make a shallow indent in the center of the mash. Put into it the egg yolk, remaining semolina, the melted butter, and the potato starch. Quickly knead the whole thing with your hands to form a smooth dough.
6. In a small bowl, mix the grated mozzarella with the ricotta and Parmesan. Season with a pinch of salt.
7. Take a golf ball–size piece of the potato dough and shape it into an oblong patty. Put some of the filling in the middle and close the potato dough around the filling. Press the sides together well all around and, with slightly moistened hands, shape into a ball.
8. Bring a pot of water to a boil and generously salt. Once the water is bubbling, reduce the heat to low. Carefully add the filled dumpling and leave to soak in the hot water for 8 minutes. Remove with a slotted spoon and let drain briefly.
9. Place the rice flour in a deep plate and roll the spider eggs all around in it. Shake off the excess flour and serve with a pretty ugly, bright green pesto or roasted vegetables.

Shrunken Potato Heads

Shrunken heads serve not only as a magical ingredient or stairwell adornment but also sometimes work as conductors! Perhaps you'll spot one hanging from a rear-view mirror.

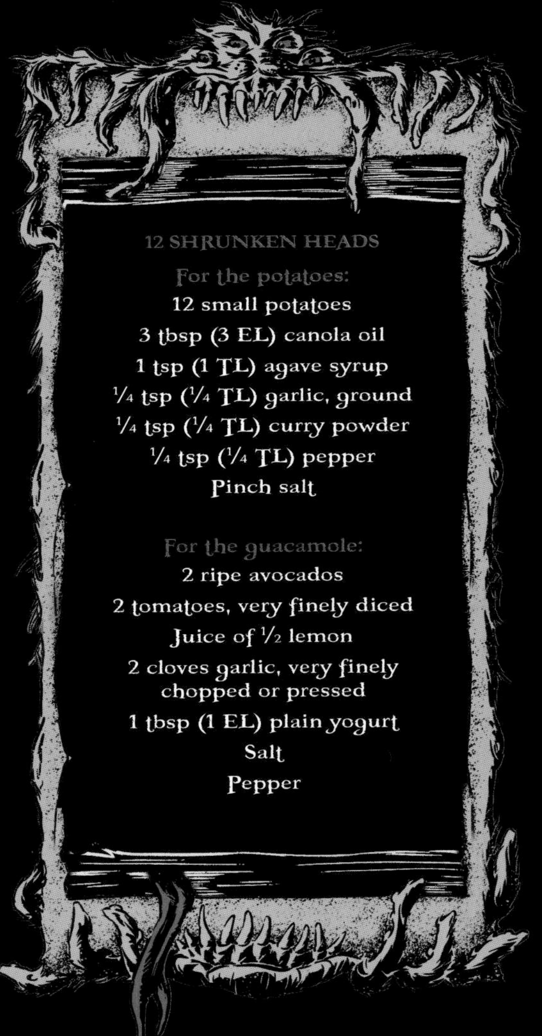

12 SHRUNKEN HEADS

For the potatoes:

12 small potatoes
3 tbsp (3 EL) canola oil
1 tsp (1 TL) agave syrup
1/4 tsp (1/4 TL) garlic, ground
1/4 tsp (1/4 TL) curry powder
1/4 tsp (1/4 TL) pepper
Pinch salt

For the guacamole:

2 ripe avocados
2 tomatoes, very finely diced
Juice of 1/2 lemon
2 cloves garlic, very finely chopped or pressed
1 tbsp (1 EL) plain yogurt
Salt
Pepper

Prepare the potatoes:

1. Wash the potatoes thoroughly, dry them, and use a small, sharp knife to carve eerie faces into them.
2. Preheat the oven to 390°F (200°C), and line a baking sheet with parchment paper.
3. In a small bowl, mix the canola oil with the agave syrup, garlic, curry powder, pepper, and salt. Generously brush the potatoes all over with it using a pastry brush. Place on the prepared baking sheet and bake in the preheated oven for about 45 minutes until golden brown. In the meantime, prepare the dip.

Prepare the guacamole:

4. Carefully halve the avocados and remove the pit. Scoop the inside out of the skin with a spoon and mash finely with a fork in a small bowl. Add the diced tomatoes, lemon juice, garlic, and yogurt and mix everything together. Season with salt and pepper. Refrigerate until ready to serve!

Stuffed Cockroaches

Dried cockroaches are a popular candy in the magical world, available for sale, along with other treats. Some have a particular fondness for these, but most people find the taste rather disgusting. It seems they haven't tried this particular variety yet!

10 COCKROACHES

10 soft dates, dried

10 tsp (10 TL) peanut butter

2.8 oz (80 g) dark chocolate, coarsely chopped

10 pecans

20 dried pine needles

Also needed: a pin

1. Carefully cut the dried dates and remove the pits; making sure that the fruit's underside remains intact!
2. Place 1 teaspoon (1 TL) of peanut butter in the center of each date and gently squeeze together the top of the fruit. Put in the refrigerator.
3. In a small, heat-resistant bowl over a saucepan of simmering water, melt the dark chocolate until thin enough to make a coating, ensuring that the bottom of the bowl does not touch the water!
4. Remove the stuffed dates from the refrigerator and dip them into the melted chocolate to evenly coat them all over. Then place a pecan on each date, press lightly, and place back in the refrigerator until the chocolate has set (about 15 minutes).
5. When the chocolate has set, use a pin to carefully poke two small holes in the head of each cockroach, and insert a dried pine needle into each hole like an antenna. Store in a cool place until ready for consumption.

The pine needles shouldn't actually be eaten, but don't worry: Unless you're eating half a Christmas tree, they're perfectly safe!

Witch Hats

Although the truth is that witches are very different from the malicious, warty hags we see in fairy tales, they otherwise do everything you'd expect them to: They fly on broomsticks, brew potions—and wear weird pointy hats. Like this one. Only bigger. And not quite as tasty.

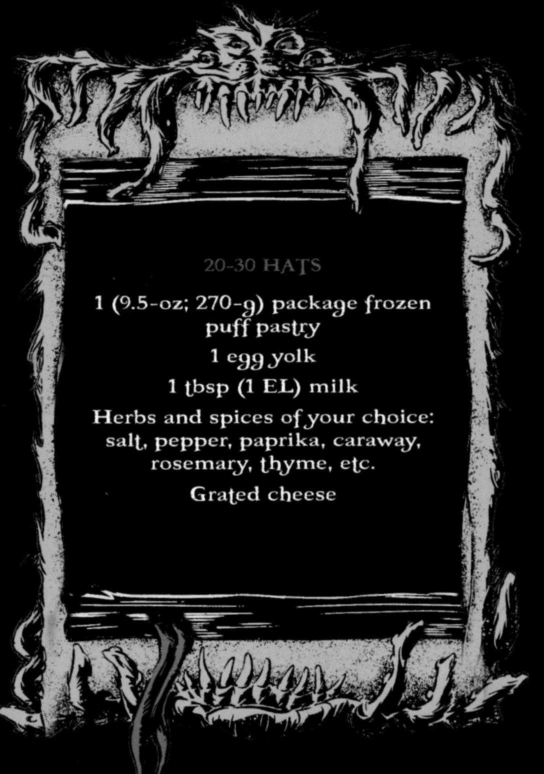

20–30 HATS

1 (9.5-oz; 270-g) package frozen puff pastry

1 egg yolk

1 tbsp (1 EL) milk

Herbs and spices of your choice: salt, pepper, paprika, caraway, rosemary, thyme, etc.

Grated cheese

1. Preheat the oven to 390°F (200°C). Line a baking sheet with parchment paper.
2. Take the puff pastry dough out and let it thaw for 10 minutes. Then roll it out on the work surface and cut in half lengthwise. Cut small triangles out of the long rectangles. Place them on the baking sheet with the point facing up and roll up the bottom edge a little. Carefully shape the resulting hats with your fingers (e.g. bend the tip of the hat a little, pull the brim down a little on the sides, etc.).
3. In a small bowl, whisk the egg yolk with the milk. Brush the hats with it, sprinkle with spices and herbs if you like, spread some grated cheese on top, and bake in the preheated oven for 15 minutes. Then take them out and let them cool down a bit on the baking sheet.

These witch hats are wonderful as an accompaniment to soup or salad, but also as a hearty go-to with wine or as a snack for the next Death Day celebration!

Gravestone Cake with Tar Glaze

I mean, maybe your friends don't eat headstones, but mine do. This recipe not only looks iconic, but is also characterized by other qualities, such as the full-bodied, elegant tar taste. Try for yourself!

1 CAKE

1¾ sticks (200 g) soft butter, plus a little more for greasing the springform pan

3.5 oz (100 g) dark chocolate, coarsely chopped

¾ cup (170 g) sugar

4 eggs

7 oz (200 g) sour cream

2 cups (250 g) flour

2 tsp (2 TL) baking powder

Pinch salt

2 tbsp (2 EL) cocoa powder

12.3 oz (350 g) sour cherries (from jar/can), drained

1¾ cups (400 ml) whipped cream, cold

2 packets (0.35 each) cream stabilizer

2 tsp (2 TL) vanilla sugar

Black food coloring

Dark chocolate sauce, to taste

Also needed: a rectangular springform pan (11 × 7½ inches; 28 × 19 cm)

1. Preheat the oven to 355°F (180°C). Line a baking sheet with parchment paper and place a springform pan on top. Generously grease the springform pan with butter.
2. Melt the dark chocolate, using a bain-marie. In a separate bowl, mix the butter with the sugar. Gradually add the eggs and stir. Add the sour cream and work it in. In a third bowl, mix the flour with the baking powder, salt, and cocoa. Then add to the butter and sour cream mixture. Mix well. Then fold in the melted chocolate and carefully drained cherries.
3. Place the dough in the springform pan and smooth the top. Bake in the preheated oven for about 50 to 55 minutes or until a toothpick inserted into the center comes out clean. Then remove from the oven and let cool. Remove the springform pan. Then chill in the refrigerator until ready to decorate.
4. In a mixing bowl, whip the cold whipped cream with the cream stabilizer and the vanilla sugar until it forms stiff peaks. Stir in a few drops of black food coloring until the cream turns a pretty tombstone gray. Pour the dyed whipped cream onto the cake and use a spatula to spread it evenly over the top and sides. Let dark chocolate sauce run over the gravestone as tar.

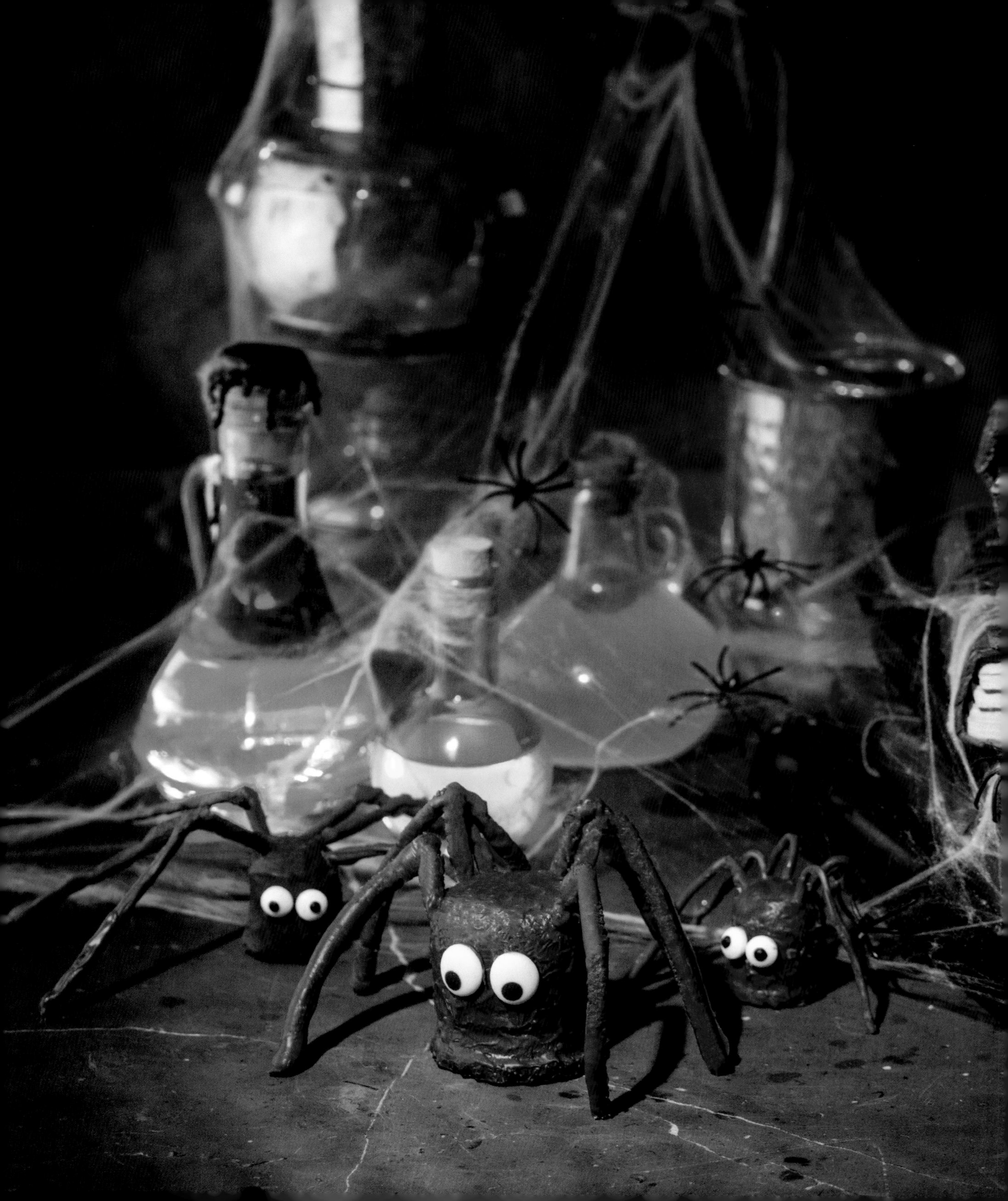

Chocolate Tarantulas

Everyone hates spiders—no clue why. I think these cute little creatures are completely misunderstood. Sure, they have eight legs and countless compound eyes, and they slurp up their paralyzed prey like fruit juice bags. But apart from that, they are quite charming creatures, and incredibly tasty at that. Their offspring in particular are considered a delicacy in many places, and rightly so, as this recipe impressively proves!

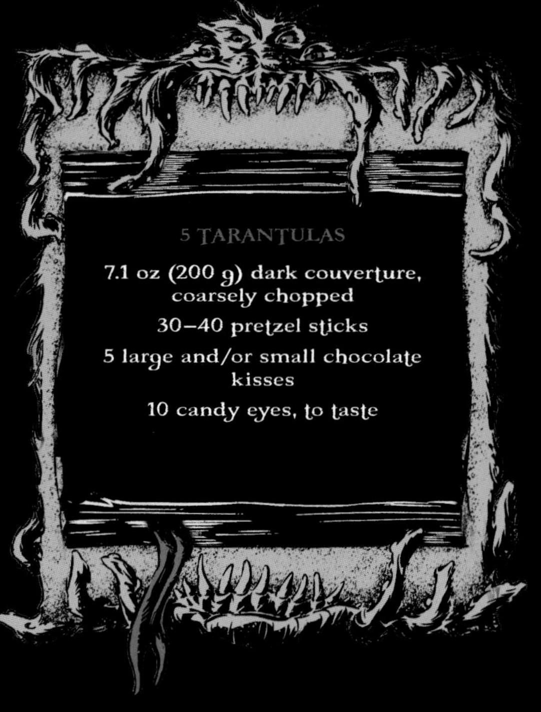

5 TARANTULAS

7.1 oz (200 g) dark couverture, coarsely chopped

30–40 pretzel sticks

5 large and/or small chocolate kisses

10 candy eyes, to taste

1. Line a baking sheet or board with parchment paper.
2. Using a bain-marie, melt the coarsely chopped chocolate for the coating. Make sure not to let the bottom of the bowl touch the boiling water.
3. Carefully break the pretzel sticks so that you get a shorter piece and a much longer one. Stick these two pieces together using the melted chocolate to create a bent spider leg. The best way to do this is to place the pretzel sticks on the baking sheet, cover the pretzel sticks completely with chocolate and carefully set the joint, pressing it in place until the adhesive has dried. Then carefully turn the spider leg and cover the other side with chocolate. Let dry completely.
4. Now prepare the chocolate kisses. To do this, use a slightly warmed, pointed knife or heat the point on a can opener to very carefully melt holes in the chocolate coating at the points where the spider legs will be attached afterward (three on each side). Then stick the shorter parts of the dried jointed spider legs into the holes and carefully adhere in place with melted chocolate. Let harden on the baking sheet in the refrigerator.
5. Then melt the remaining chocolate coating again and brush the spiders all over with it, using a small pastry brush, to give the tarantulas a little more texture. Finally, carefully place two candy eyes on the still moist chocolate and allow to dry. Keep refrigerated until ready to eat.

Bat Blood Soup

Bats are highly sought after by spellcasters, as their spleen is a key ingredient in many magical remedies. And there are numerous uses for the bloodsuckers' blood. One is as follows: You can make a delicious soup out of it! The effect of consuming it has not yet been sufficiently researched scientifically, but one thing is certain: This soup is addictive! After the first spoonful, you always want more. So be sure to eat it prudently!

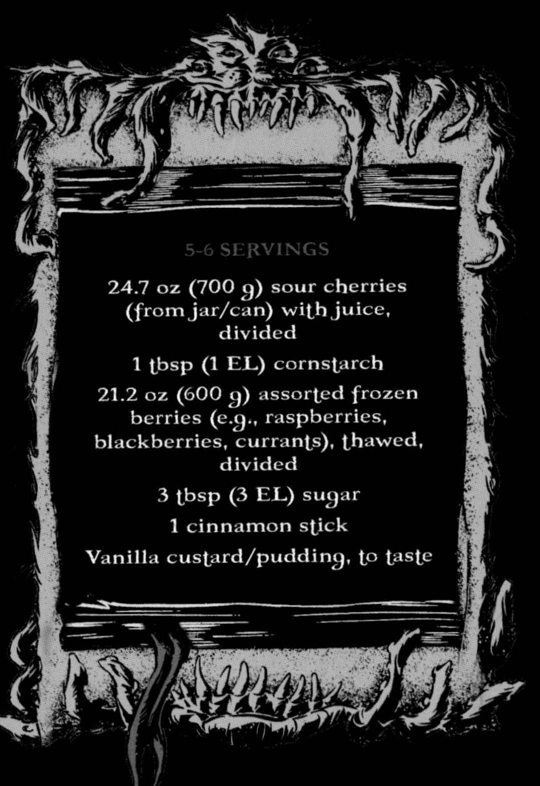

5-6 SERVINGS
24.7 oz (700 g) sour cherries (from jar/can) with juice, divided
1 tbsp (1 EL) cornstarch
21.2 oz (600 g) assorted frozen berries (e.g., raspberries, blackberries, currants), thawed, divided
3 tbsp (3 EL) sugar
1 cinnamon stick
Vanilla custard/pudding, to taste

1. Strain the cherries through a sieve, collecting the juice.
2. In a small bowl, mix 3 tablespoons (3 EL) of the cherry juice with the cornstarch and set aside. Put the remaining cherry juice, 14.1 ounces (400 g) of the defrosted frozen berries, the sugar, and the cinnamon stick in a saucepan over medium heat and simmer, stirring constantly, until the berries gradually fall apart (5 minutes). Then remove from the heat, take out the cinnamon stick, and carefully chop the berries with an immersion blender. If you want a very fine puree, strain it through a sieve. Then put it back into the pot.
3. Thoroughly stir the mixed starch again, then put it together with the berry puree. Put the pot back on the stove, bring the puree to a boil, and simmer over low heat for about 5 minutes, stirring regularly. Add the sour cherries and the remaining berries and bring everything to boil again. Remove from the heat and let the porridge cool to room temperature. Then place in the refrigerator for 4 hours.
4. Pour the blood soup into glasses or dessert bowls and serve warm or cold. Best served with vanilla custard or pudding.

Raven Charred Pastries and Very Moldy Cheese

This is one classic that a book of recipes for the spookiest celebration of the year couldn't be without! The decisive factor here is to forget about the baked goods in the oven at a high temperature for as long as possible and to lay out the cheese for aging in a damp, dark place months before the happy occasion, so that it is really moldy when the guests finally arrive.

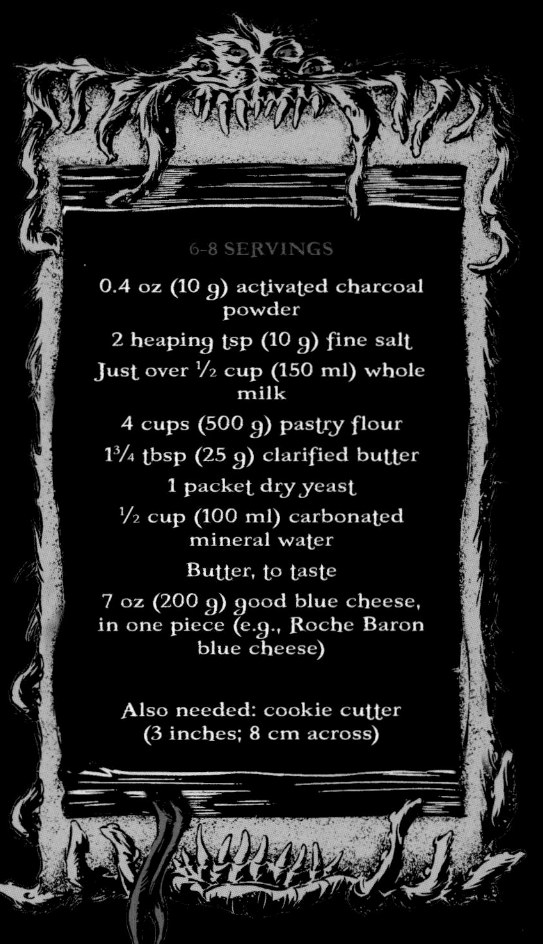

6–8 SERVINGS

0.4 oz (10 g) activated charcoal powder

2 heaping tsp (10 g) fine salt

Just over ½ cup (150 ml) whole milk

4 cups (500 g) pastry flour

1¾ tbsp (25 g) clarified butter

1 packet dry yeast

½ cup (100 ml) carbonated mineral water

Butter, to taste

7 oz (200 g) good blue cheese, in one piece (e.g., Roche Baron blue cheese)

Also needed: cookie cutter (3 inches; 8 cm across)

1. In a small bowl, stir together the activated charcoal, salt, and milk. Let sit for 10 minutes.
2. In a separate bowl, mix together the flour, clarified butter, and dry yeast. Pour in the mineral water, mix everything thoroughly, and knead with your hands until you have a soft, elastic dough. Form a ball, cover with a clean dish towel, and let rise in a warm place for at least an hour.
3. Then roll out the dough with a rolling pin on a lightly floured surface to about .4 inch (1 cm) thick. Using a cookie cutter, cut out as many circles of dough as possible. Knead the remaining dough again, roll out again, and cut out more circles until all the dough is used up. Cover the dough slices with a clean dish towel and let them rise again for 30 minutes.
4. Brush a nonstick frying pan lightly with butter, heat over medium heat, and cook the dough slices for 2 to 3 minutes per side. Place the finished pastry on a plate lined with kitchen paper to drain and repeat the process until all the pastry slices are used up.
5. Best served warm with some butter and a piece of good blue cheese!

Stuffed Shrunken Heads

Shrunken heads are not uncommon in the wizarding world. They can be used for decorations or ingredients in rather questionable potions. So far, however, no one has come up with the idea of eating these magically preserved little things. The preparation options are almost endless: they can be steamed, boiled, roasted, stewed, and stuffed with all kinds of delicacies, just like in this recipe.

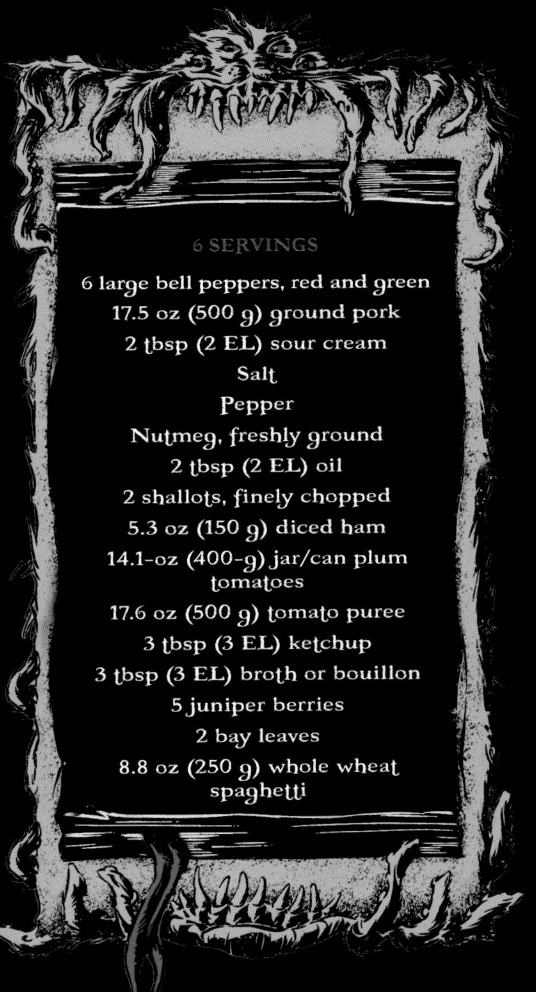

6 SERVINGS

6 large bell peppers, red and green
17.5 oz (500 g) ground pork
2 tbsp (2 EL) sour cream
Salt
Pepper
Nutmeg, freshly ground
2 tbsp (2 EL) oil
2 shallots, finely chopped
5.3 oz (150 g) diced ham
14.1-oz (400-g) jar/can plum tomatoes
17.6 oz (500 g) tomato puree
3 tbsp (3 EL) ketchup
3 tbsp (3 EL) broth or bouillon
5 juniper berries
2 bay leaves
8.8 oz (250 g) whole wheat spaghetti

1. Preheat the oven to 355°F (180°C).
2. Wash the peppers and pat dry with paper towels. Using a sharp knife, cut off the tops and stems and set aside. Remove the seeds and pith from inside the peppers. Use a small, sharp knife to carve ghastly faces into the peppers.
3. Mix the ground pork with the sour cream in a bowl and season with pepper, salt, and a little nutmeg. Fill the hollowed-out peppers to the maximum with the ground pork and smooth off the top.
4. Heat the oil in a pan over medium heat. Add the shallots and sauté until translucent (about 2 to 3 minutes). Add the diced ham and sauté. Add the plum tomatoes, tomato puree, ketchup, bouillon, juniper berries, and bay leaves, bring to a simmer, then simmer for five minutes, stirring constantly. Then pour into a casserole dish and mix well. Finally, submerge the stuffed peppers into the tomato sauce so that they are almost completely covered. Place on the oven's middle rack to cook for about 45 to 50 minutes. During this time, pour the sauce over the peppers regularly so they don't dry out.
5. About 15 minutes before the shrunken heads finish cooking, prepare the whole wheat pasta according to the package instructions. Drain thoroughly.
6. As soon as the peppers are cooked through, arrange the whole wheat spaghetti on deep plates and set a shrunken head on each. Remove the bay leaves and juniper berries from the sauce and discard these. Thoroughly stir the tomato sauce and pour it generously over the shrunken heads. Serve immediately.

Spoiled Fish

If your friends don't eat the spoiled fish you serve them at your Halloween gathering, are they even really your friends? I didn't think so.

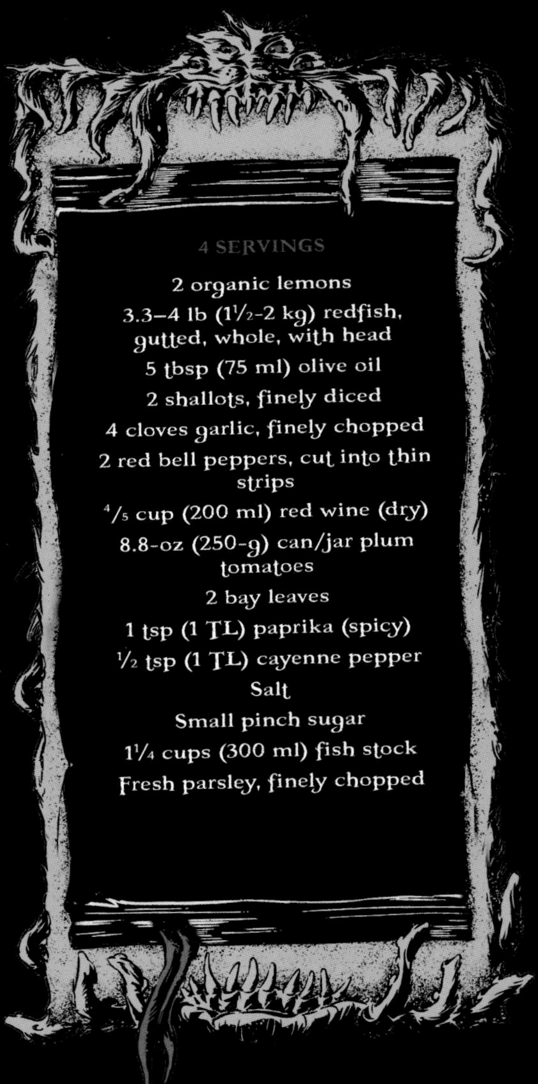

4 SERVINGS
2 organic lemons
3.3–4 lb (1½–2 kg) redfish, gutted, whole, with head
5 tbsp (75 ml) olive oil
2 shallots, finely diced
4 cloves garlic, finely chopped
2 red bell peppers, cut into thin strips
⅘ cup (200 ml) red wine (dry)
8.8-oz (250-g) can/jar plum tomatoes
2 bay leaves
1 tsp (1 TL) paprika (spicy)
½ tsp (1 TL) cayenne pepper
Salt
Small pinch sugar
1¼ cups (300 ml) fish stock
Fresh parsley, finely chopped

1. Wash the lemons thoroughly. Zest one of the lemons. Squeeze the juice from both lemons. Brush the cleaned fish generously inside and outside with the lemon juice. Set aside.
2. In a large casserole dish over high heat, warm the oil. Add the shallots and sauté until translucent. Briefly sweat the garlic and the diced peppers. Deglaze with the red wine. Add the plum tomatoes, bay leaves, and spicy paprika, and season with the cayenne pepper, salt, and sugar. Pour in the fish stock and cook over medium heat, simmering for 5 minutes.
3. Remove the bay leaves. Salt the fish inside and out, place it whole in the sauce so that it gets completely covered by the liquid, and simmer gently for about 30 minutes. Season to taste, fold in some parsley, sprinkle with more freshly chopped parsley, and serve with bread or rice.

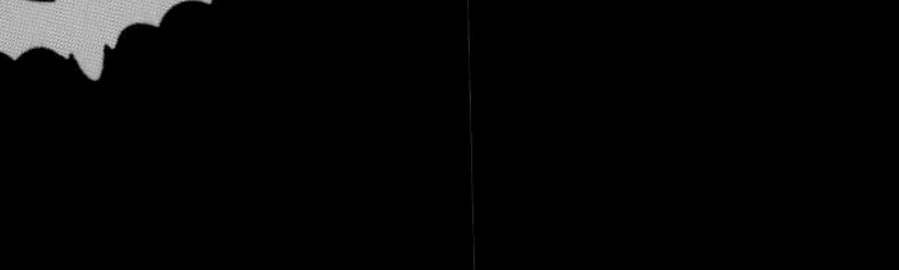

Slime-Covered Giant Spider Eggs.

A giant spider naturally lays a huge number of eggs—which can be prepared in so many different ways that you could produce an entire cookbook just on that. (And a thick one at that.) Anyway, this is my spider recipe #32991, a.k.a. Slime-Covered Giant Spider Eggs. Well, then: Bon appétit!

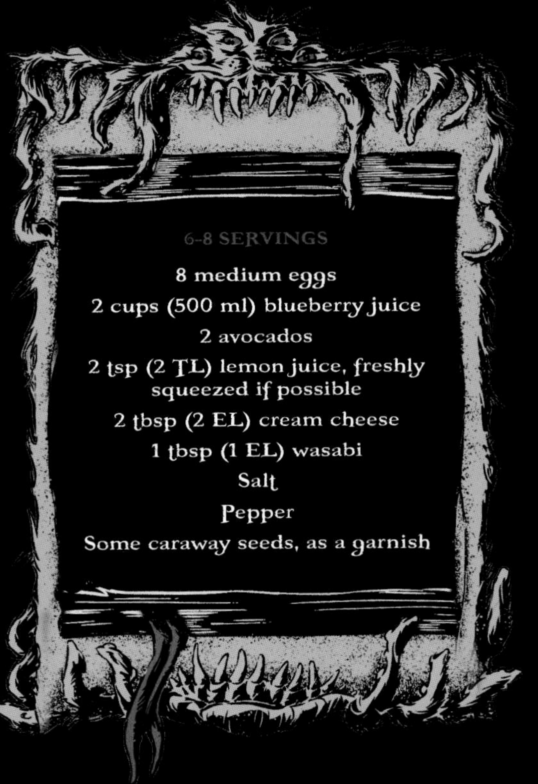

6–8 SERVINGS

8 medium eggs

2 cups (500 ml) blueberry juice

2 avocados

2 tsp (2 TL) lemon juice, freshly squeezed if possible

2 tbsp (2 EL) cream cheese

1 tbsp (1 EL) wasabi

Salt

Pepper

Some caraway seeds, as a garnish

1. Bring water to a boil in a medium saucepan. Add the eggs and hard-boil for 8–10 minutes. Drain the water and then put the eggs in a bowl of ice-cold water. Take the eggs out, pat dry with paper towels, and gently hit them all around with a tablespoon so that the shell develops fine cracks.
2. Pour the blueberry juice into a bowl and carefully place the eggs inside so that they are completely covered by the juice. Place in the refrigerator for at least 3 or 4 hours, preferably overnight, to allow the juice to soak in properly.
3. Take the eggs out of the juice, pat dry with a paper towel, and peel. The eggs are now covered with fine, dark veins. Cut the eggs in half with a very sharp knife and carefully remove the yolk with a spoon.
4. Put the yolk in a small bowl. Cut the avocado in half and scoop out the flesh with a spoon. Add the avocado flesh to the bowl along with the lemon juice, cream cheese and wasabi and puree everything finely with an immersion blender. Season with salt and pepper.
5. Place the guacamole cream in a piping bag and carefully fill the hollowed-out egg halves. (Alternatively, simply cut off a small corner from a freezer bag and use this to pipe in the guacamole cream.) Sprinkle black caraway seeds sparingly over the filling and arrange on a large serving plate.

Of course, you can use other colored liquids instead of blueberry juice, such as beet juice, cherry juice, or simply water with food coloring. The key is that the eggs end up looking appropriately . . . monstrous! By the way, afterward the juice can still be drunk without hesitation and tastes the same as before!

RIP
TOM
RIDDLE

Graveyard Rocks

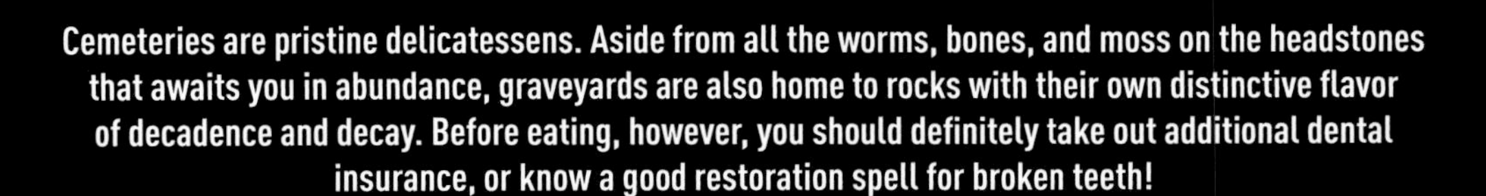

Cemeteries are pristine delicatessens. Aside from all the worms, bones, and moss on the headstones that awaits you in abundance, graveyards are also home to rocks with their own distinctive flavor of decadence and decay. Before eating, however, you should definitely take out additional dental insurance, or know a good restoration spell for broken teeth!

MORE THAN 12 ROCKS

4/5 cup (200 ml) sweetened condensed milk

12 oz (340 g) white chocolate, coarsely chopped

3.5 oz (100 g) chocolate cookie crumbs

Black food coloring or cocoa powder

1/4 cup (30 g) whole almonds

1. In a small saucepan over low heat, combine the condensed milk and chopped white chocolate. Heat for several minutes, stirring occasionally, until the chocolate is half-melted, then remove from the heat and continue stirring until smooth and malleable.
2. Stir in the cookie crumbs and evenly divide the mixture between three bowls. Add as much food coloring or cocoa powder to each bowl as needed to get different shades of gray and black. Let the mixture cool enough so that you can work with it without burning your fingers. Then take small spoonfuls of the mixture from the bowl and use to adhere the almonds together and shape into a rough stone. Place on a baking sheet lined with parchment paper and allow to cool completely. Store in an airtight sealable container.

Bowl of Fire

Only hell burns hotter than this. You've been warned.

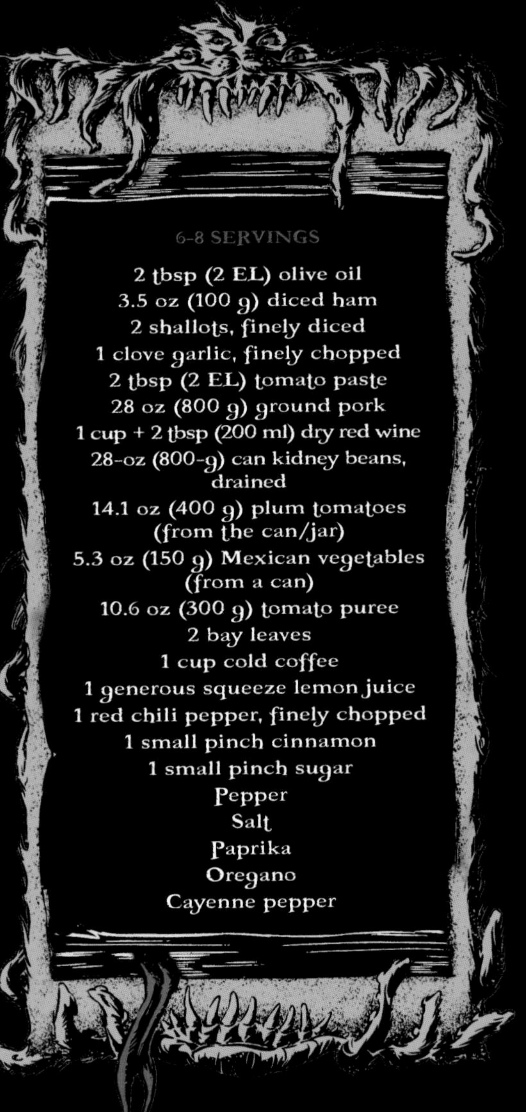

6-8 SERVINGS

2 tbsp (2 EL) olive oil
3.5 oz (100 g) diced ham
2 shallots, finely diced
1 clove garlic, finely chopped
2 tbsp (2 EL) tomato paste
28 oz (800 g) ground pork
1 cup + 2 tbsp (200 ml) dry red wine
28-oz (800-g) can kidney beans, drained
14.1 oz (400 g) plum tomatoes (from the can/jar)
5.3 oz (150 g) Mexican vegetables (from a can)
10.6 oz (300 g) tomato puree
2 bay leaves
1 cup cold coffee
1 generous squeeze lemon juice
1 red chili pepper, finely chopped
1 small pinch cinnamon
1 small pinch sugar
Pepper
Salt
Paprika
Oregano
Cayenne pepper

1. In a large saucepan over medium heat, heat the olive oil. Add the diced ham and sear. Add the shallots and garlic and heat until translucent. Stir in the tomato paste and cook until the meat starts browning. Add the ground pork, mix well, and sear on all sides, stirring occasionally. Deglaze with the red wine.
2. Put the kidney beans, the plum tomatoes, and the Mexican vegetables in the pot together, along with the tomato puree and the bay leaves. Pour in a cup of cold coffee, stir well, and simmer over low heat for 20 minutes, stirring occasionally.
3. After the cooking time ends, remove the bay leaves, add the lemon juice, finely chopped chili pepper and cinnamon. Stir in a small pinch of sugar. Season to taste with pepper, salt, oregano, paprika, and cayenne pepper. But be careful with the spiciness: it's better to add more seasoning than risk making the whole thing too fiery!

ATIUS BORAGE'S
DVANCED
POTION
MAKIN

Eyeball Punch

No Halloween celebration would be complete without a proper punch, and this is the ideal refreshment on a sweltering summer evening or for an office outing to hell. Most of the ingredients are easy to get. Well, the spider eyes for this are a bit harder to get, as the beasts won't give up their peepers willingly to save their lives, even though they have more than enough of them! But believe me: it's worth the effort!

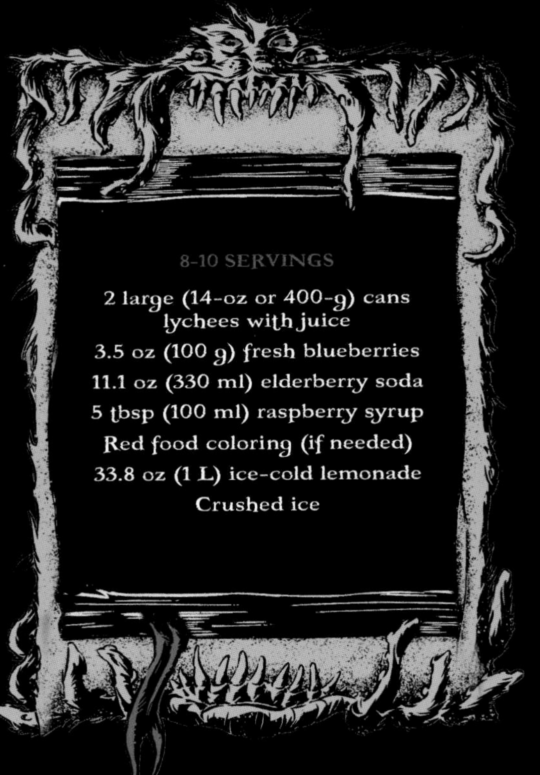

8–10 SERVINGS

2 large (14-oz or 400-g) cans lychees with juice
3.5 oz (100 g) fresh blueberries
11.1 oz (330 ml) elderberry soda
5 tbsp (100 ml) raspberry syrup
Red food coloring (if needed)
33.8 oz (1 L) ice-cold lemonade
Crushed ice

1. Drain the lychees through a colander, saving the juice. Stick an adequately sized blueberry into the hole of each lychee to serve as an iris. You'll have a batch of ghastly authentic eyeballs in no time!
2. Pour the lychee juice into a punch bowl. Add the elderberry soda and raspberry syrup and mix well. Should it not look bloody enough, stir in some red food coloring.
3. Carefully place the eyes in the bowl, stir gently, cover with plastic wrap, and leave in the refrigerator for 2 or 3 hours. Then the eyes will float on top and will be crisscrossed by little red veins. Carefully pour in the ice-cold lemonade and stir gently.
4. Add some crushed ice to the punch before serving.

If you prefer a tastier eyeball punch, you can simply replace the lemonade with grapefruit wheat beer and add ½ cup (100 ml) of apple schnapps or vodka. That will cheer up even the grimmest house ghost!

Pumpkin Soup

If there's one thing inextricably linked to the year's spookiest holiday, it's pumpkin soup. No surprise there: nothing looks more unappetizing than this viscous, orange-yellow goop, which to top it all off is terribly healthy.

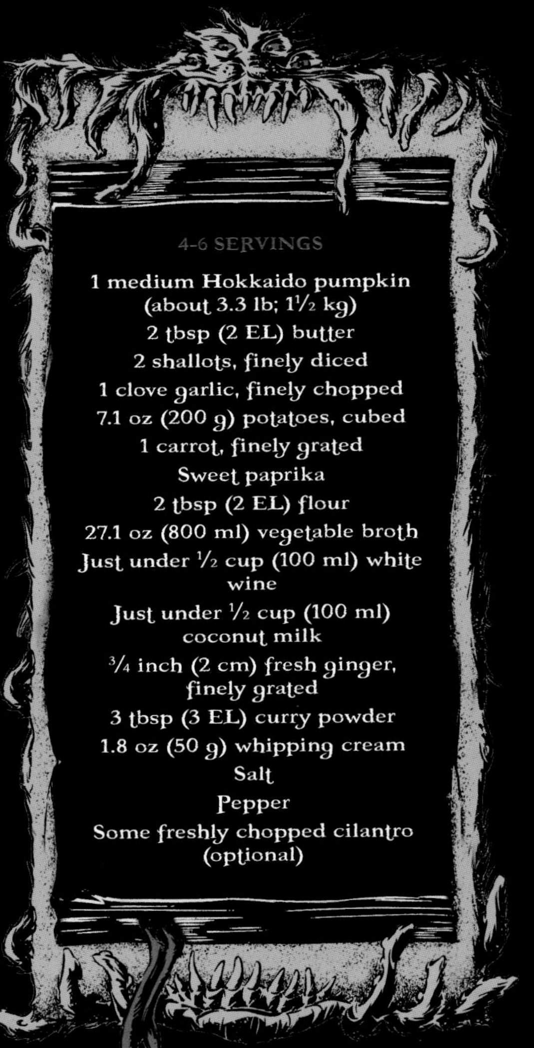

4–6 SERVINGS

1 medium Hokkaido pumpkin (about 3.3 lb; 1½ kg)
2 tbsp (2 EL) butter
2 shallots, finely diced
1 clove garlic, finely chopped
7.1 oz (200 g) potatoes, cubed
1 carrot, finely grated
Sweet paprika
2 tbsp (2 EL) flour
27.1 oz (800 ml) vegetable broth
Just under ½ cup (100 ml) white wine
Just under ½ cup (100 ml) coconut milk
¾ inch (2 cm) fresh ginger, finely grated
3 tbsp (3 EL) curry powder
1.8 oz (50 g) whipping cream
Salt
Pepper
Some freshly chopped cilantro (optional)

1. Preheat the oven to 175°F (80°C). Line a baking sheet with parchment paper.
2. Wash and quarter the pumpkin. Carefully scrape out the seeds and pulp with a tablespoon and discard. Coarsely chop the pumpkin and skin, place on the baking sheet, and cook in the oven for 20 minutes. Then remove, drain excess liquid, and set aside.
3. In a large saucepan over medium-high heat, heat the butter. Sweat the shallots and garlic until translucent. Add the pumpkin pieces and sauté briefly. Add the potatoes and grated carrots, sprinkle with paprika and the flour, and mix everything together. Then pour in the vegetable broth, white wine, and coconut milk. Bring to a boil briefly and simmer, covered, over low heat for 25 minutes, stirring occasionally.
4. Add the grated ginger and curry powder. Carefully puree the soup in a saucepan using an immersion blender, add the cream, and season generously with salt and pepper. Serve sprinkled with some freshly chopped cilantro on top, to taste.

You can also easily leave out the white wine without any issue. However, you should then add a dash of vinegar to the soup to give the dish a certain acidity. Because you know: a dash of sour makes it sweet!

Restoration Potion

A well-intentioned forewarning: This nasty concoction is impossible to make without alcohol! So either you do it right or just leave it alone, as is. No going only halfway. It's like being dead. Especially since you're killing two cemetery crows with one stone: should you break your bones under the intoxicating influence of this brew, they'll grow right back together! Really handy!

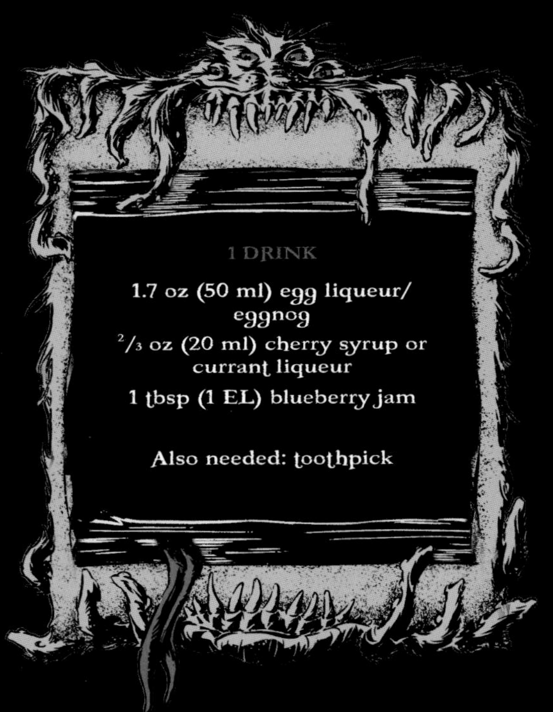

1 DRINK

1.7 oz (50 ml) egg liqueur/eggnog

$^2/_3$ oz (20 ml) cherry syrup or currant liqueur

1 tbsp (1 EL) blueberry jam

Also needed: toothpick

1. Pour the egg liqueur or eggnog into a champagne glass. Carefully pour half of the cherry syrup or currant liqueur into the middle of the egg liqueur/eggnog.
2. Mix the remaining syrup or liqueur with the blueberry jam in a small bowl and carefully pour into the middle of the eggnog. Then pull a toothpick through the glass so that blood-red streaks appear as veins in the potion. Serve immediately!

Witches' Brooms

Nowadays, at least one flying broomstick can be found in every wizarding household, as it's common for the magically inclined to use these handy craft for just about anything from sports to a morning flight to the witches' market. But while current models have all sorts of functions, the first flying brooms were quite uncomfortable and only had simple control features—which is sometimes totally sufficient. Like with these brooms, which have only one goal anyway: to land in your mouth!

10 WITCHES' BROOMS

10 chives

5 slices Gouda (or your preference of another pliable round cheese)

10 salami sticks, as thin as possible

1. Place the chives in a bowl, pour boiling water over them, and let sit for 5 minutes. Drain and place the chives on a plate lined with paper towels to dry.
2. Lay the cheese slices on top of each other and cut in half lengthwise, or in such a way that the proportioning fits the salami sticks you are using. Then, on a cutting board, cut the cheese slices on one side at regular intervals of 1/8 inch (5 mm); leave about ¾ inch (2 cm) space to the top edge.
3. Place the salami sticks on the uncut end of the cheese slices and carefully wrap the cheese around them. Wrap in place with a blanched chives and tie carefully. Trim the excess chives with scissors.

Pumpkin
juice

Pumpkin Juice

If you love pumpkins as much as some wizards in training do, the smell of this juice will perk you right up!

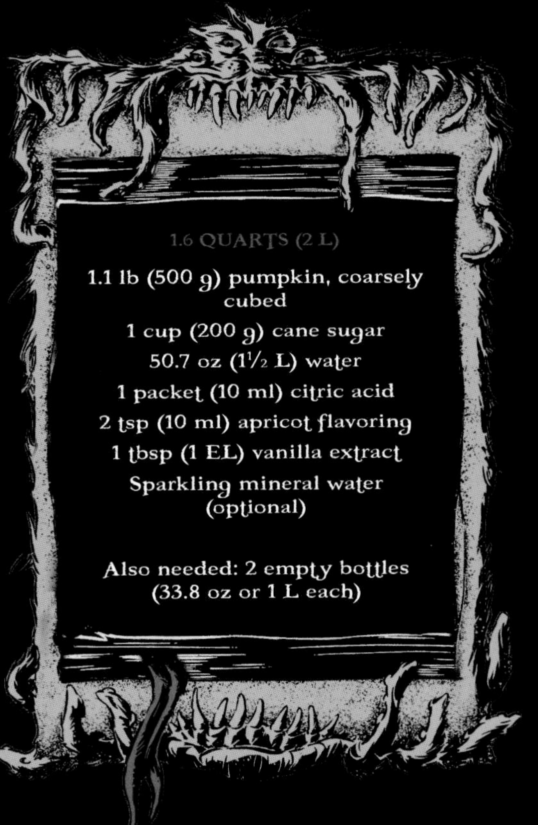

1.6 QUARTS (2 L)

1.1 lb (500 g) pumpkin, coarsely cubed

1 cup (200 g) cane sugar

50.7 oz (1½ L) water

1 packet (10 ml) citric acid

2 tsp (10 ml) apricot flavoring

1 tbsp (1 EL) vanilla extract

Sparkling mineral water (optional)

Also needed: 2 empty bottles (33.8 oz or 1 L each)

1. Preheat the oven to 350°F (175°C). Line a baking sheet with parchment paper.
2. Wrap the pumpkin cubes in aluminum foil and place on the baking sheet. Cook in the oven for about 20 minutes until the pumpkin is soft and the skin can be easily separated from the flesh. Then put the pumpkin flesh in a bowl and puree it finely with an immersion blender.
3. Place the pumpkin puree in a large saucepan along with the sugar and water. Bring to a boil and simmer over low heat for about 20 minutes, stirring constantly. Stir in the citric acid, the apricot flavoring, and the vanilla, mix everything well, and pour into both empty bottles, which have already been rinsed with hot water. Seal the bottles and store in the refrigerator. If chilled, the pumpkin juice will keep well for 3 or 4 days.
4. If you find the pumpkin juice is too thick, mix it with some carbonated mineral water immediately before serving!

Unlike most other pumpkin juice recipes, this one is sweet instead of savory and tastes best chilled!

Maggot Loaf

Admittedly, this recipe is not for the faint of heart or those reluctant to experiment with new foods. But if you let the stuff sit for a few months, at least the maggots will enjoy it.

4 SERVINGS

1 sheep stomach
1 sheep kidney
1 sheep heart
1 sheep lung
1 bay leaf
4 juniper berries
1 clove
2 onions, finely diced
2½ cups (200 g) oatmeal
1 sheep liver
3.5 oz (100 g) suet
Salt
Pepper
Pinch nutmeg
Pinch cayenne pepper
Cooked rice, to taste

Also needed: sewing needle, kitchen twine

1. Wash the sheep's stomach carefully; remove the flaps of skin and fat and soak the stomach in cold salt water overnight. Then turn inside out, wash thoroughly and carefully scrape the insides of the stomach with the blunt side of a knife.
2. Place the kidney, heart, and lungs in a large saucepan and cover with cold, heavily salted water. Add the bay leaf, juniper berries, and clove, bring to a boil over medium heat, and simmer uncovered for about 1½ hours. Then remove from the heat, strain the broth through a sieve into another saucepan, and set the cooked offal aside.
3. In a pan over medium-high heat, sauté the onions and oatmeal until golden brown. Finely dice half the liver, heart, and lungs (remove the windpipe first if necessary). Coarsely chop the rest of the liver and suet and mix these together in a separate bowl.
4. Mix the cooked meat, liver, and fat blend, along with the oatmeal and onion mixture, in a large bowl and season generously with salt, pepper, nutmeg, and cayenne pepper. Gradually pour in the set aside broth, stirring constantly, until a soft mass forms.
5. Fill the washed sheep stomach with the mixture. Attention: Only fill up the stomach ⅔ of the way, as the oats expand when cooking! Then carefully press the air out of the stomach, sew up with a sewing needle and kitchen twine, and stab several times with a knife. Then cook in a large saucepan over medium-high heat, uncovered, for about 3 to 4 hours; always top up the water as it boils off.
6. Once cooked, remove the twine and arrange on a serving platter with cooked maggots, aka the white rice.

Caution: The stomach contents are under pressure! Proceed carefully when cutting open, otherwise, worst case scenario: new wallpaper will be necessary!

Ghost Posts

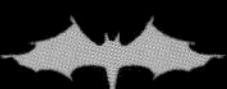

Most people are afraid of ghosts. There is absolutely no reason for this, because most ghosts are just darling. Those pictured here are the best example: totally chilled, funny to look at, and so sweet that you just have to like them!

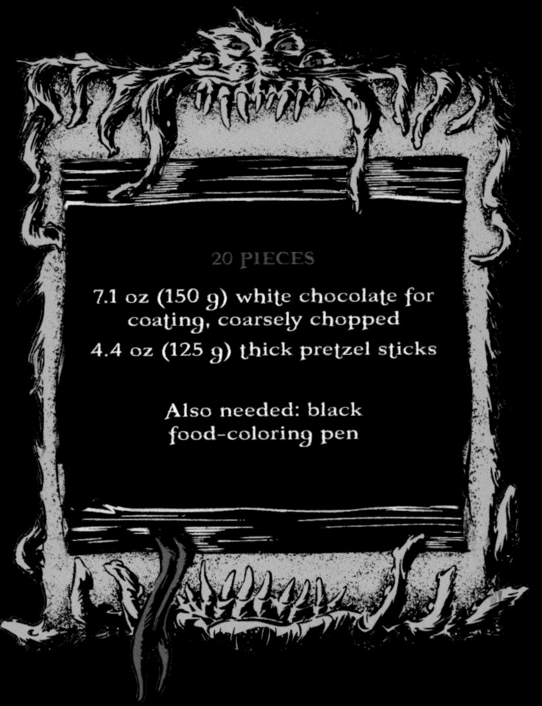

20 PIECES

7.1 oz (150 g) white chocolate for coating, coarsely chopped

4.4 oz (125 g) thick pretzel sticks

Also needed: black food-coloring pen

1. Set up a bain-marie/double boiler. To do so, put water in a saucepan, place a small metal bowl in it, and keep the stovetop on low. Then melt 2/3 of the coarsely chopped chocolate for coating in ensuring that the bottom of the bowl does not touch the water! Also, the water must not boil! Once the contents have melted completely, add the remaining chocolate and allow to cool slightly. Then carefully reheat the chocolate mass to 90°F (32°C) and remove the bowl from the bain-marie.
2. Now quickly dip the pretzel sticks into the melted chocolate, because the coating will quickly harden again as it cools. Cover the pretzel sticks about ⅔ of the way with the white chocolate and then place them upright in a glass, with the chocolate side up, and spaced far enough apart so that the ghost poles don't stick together.
3. Let the pretzel sticks dry for about 15 minutes. As soon as the chocolate has dried, draw creepy ghost faces on the coating with a black food-coloring pen.

Grilled Monster Thighs

These thighs are especially tasty! Meaty, juicy and piquantly seasoned . . . Try them and see for yourself!

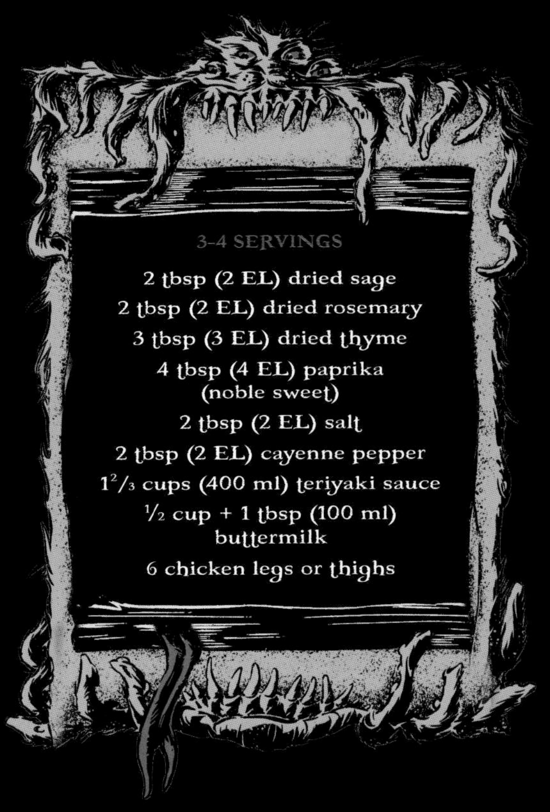

3–4 SERVINGS

2 tbsp (2 EL) dried sage
2 tbsp (2 EL) dried rosemary
3 tbsp (3 EL) dried thyme
4 tbsp (4 EL) paprika (noble sweet)
2 tbsp (2 EL) salt
2 tbsp (2 EL) cayenne pepper
1⅔ cups (400 ml) teriyaki sauce
½ cup + 1 tbsp (100 ml) buttermilk
6 chicken legs or thighs

1. In a small bowl, combine half of the sage, rosemary, thyme, paprika, salt, cayenne, teriyaki sauce, and all of the buttermilk. Pour into a sealable freezer bag.
2. Rinse the chicken thighs briefly, pat dry with dish towels, and place in the bag with the marinade. Seal the bag, massage the marinade into the meat, and then place in the refrigerator for at least 3 hours, preferably overnight.
3. Remove the chicken thighs from the marinade. Dispose of the marinade, place the remaining ingredients in a small saucepan, and reduce over medium-high heat, stirring constantly, for 30 minutes, until a nice, glossy, dark varnish forms. Remove from the stove and let cool a bit.
4. In the interim, preheat the oven to 320°F (160°C). Slide an oven rack into the middle shelf; place a large bowl underneath with a bit of water to catch any dripping fat.
5. Generously brush the chicken thighs all around with the seasoning varnish and place on the oven rack. Cover loosely with aluminum foil and cook in the oven for 40 to 45 minutes; after 20 minutes, turn and brush again with the seasoning mixture.
6. When the time's up, brush the chicken thighs with the remaining seasoning mixture, remove the aluminum foil and increase the heat to 430°F (220°C) for 5 minutes so that the skin gets nice and crispy. Then remove from the oven, arrange on a large plate, and serve immediately.

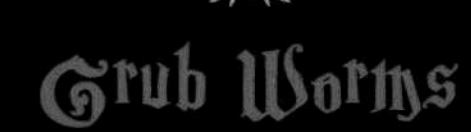

Grub Worms

Cemeteries aren't inherently particularly appetizing places. For certain ghosts and ghouls, however, they sure are. And of course for worms. They'll find plenty of delicious snacks to fill their guts with—until they end up on the menu themselves.

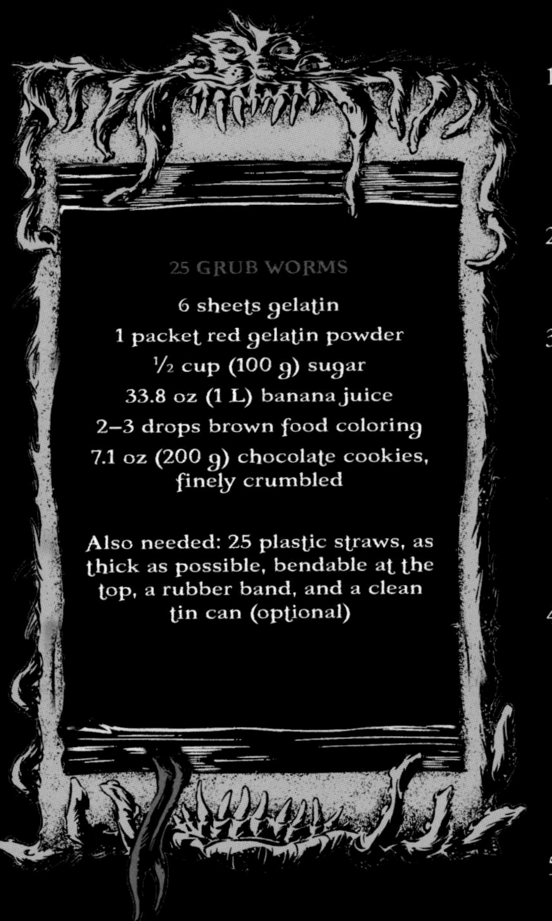

25 GRUB WORMS

6 sheets gelatin

1 packet red gelatin powder

½ cup (100 g) sugar

33.8 oz (1 L) banana juice

2–3 drops brown food coloring

7.1 oz (200 g) chocolate cookies, finely crumbled

Also needed: 25 plastic straws, as thick as possible, bendable at the top, a rubber band, and a clean tin can (optional)

1. Extend the straws to their full length at the bend and place them, ribbed side down, in a large, tall glass; use as many straws as possible until no more fit into the container. Then wrap the straws tightly with a rubber band just below the top end.
2. Soak the gelatin sheets in a bowl of cold water for a few minutes. Then drain and gently squeeze out the gelatin. Set aside.
3. Mix the gelatin powder and the sugar in a medium saucepan and pour in the banana juice, whisking constantly. Continue stirring until smooth. Stir in some brown food coloring to make the worms look real. Heat over medium-high heat, stirring regularly, until the liquid is almost boiling—but only just! Then remove from the heat and stir in the softened gelatin sheets with a whisk. Pour the gelatin into a measuring cup or other container that you can use to better measure.
4. Slowly pour the gelatin dessert into the tied straws, up to 2 inches (5 cm) below the upper edge. You don't have to fill each tube individually! It's enough if you simply pour the gelatin dessert into the middle, as the outer straws will fill up all by themselves due to the rising liquid level at the bottom of the glass. Then chill the straws in the refrigerator for at least 8 hours, preferably overnight.
5. Remove from the refrigerator, remove the rubber band, and briefly hold the straws under warm running water. Pat dry with kitchen paper and gently squeeze the worms out of the plastic tubes one by one. Mix carefully with the crumbled chocolate cookies in a bowl and serve in a thoroughly washed tin, if desired. Bon appétit!

Bloodsuckers

Be forewarned: These lollipops are real shockers—sugar shockers! Because sugar is something really bad! The opposite is the case here: Sugar is fun! Sugar brings joy! Sugar brings people together!

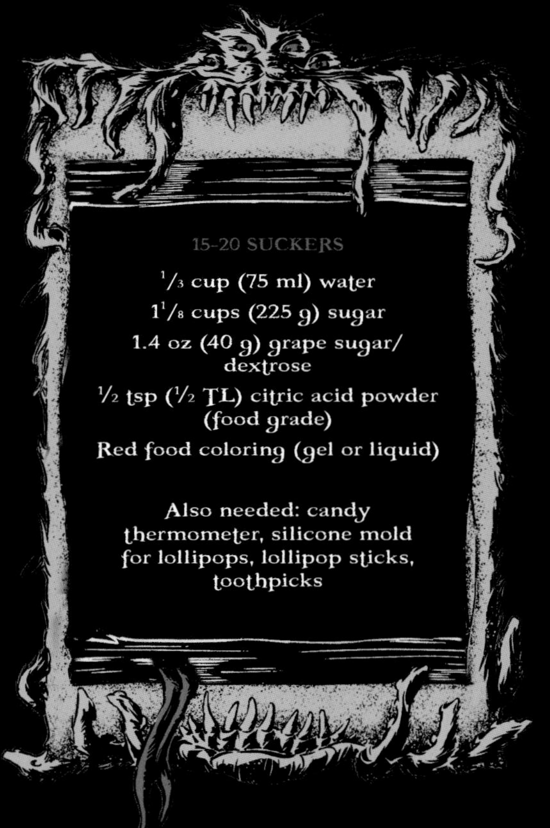

15–20 SUCKERS

$^1/_3$ cup (75 ml) water

$1^1/_8$ cups (225 g) sugar

1.4 oz (40 g) grape sugar/dextrose

½ tsp (½ TL) citric acid powder (food grade)

Red food coloring (gel or liquid)

Also needed: candy thermometer, silicone mold for lollipops, lollipop sticks, toothpicks

1. Place the lollipop sticks in the lollipop mold.
2. Place the water, sugar, and grape sugar in a small saucepan and heat over medium-high heat, stirring constantly, until the sugar has completely dissolved. Then increase the heat and stop stirring immediately. Check the temperature with the candy thermometer. When the temperature reaches 310°F (155°C), immediately remove from the heat and place on a heat-resistant surface.
3. Quickly stir in the citric acid and carefully pour the mixture into the silicone mold. Attention: Hot!
4. Dip a toothpick in the red food coloring and draw blood-red streaks in each lollipop.
5. Allow the lollipops to harden completely before releasing from the mold. These are best kept in an airtight container.

Pull-Apart Magical Bubble Bread

You'll love this enchanting recipe, ideal for savory dishes, soups, and dips. It could easily have also come from a magical cookbook, that's how good it is.

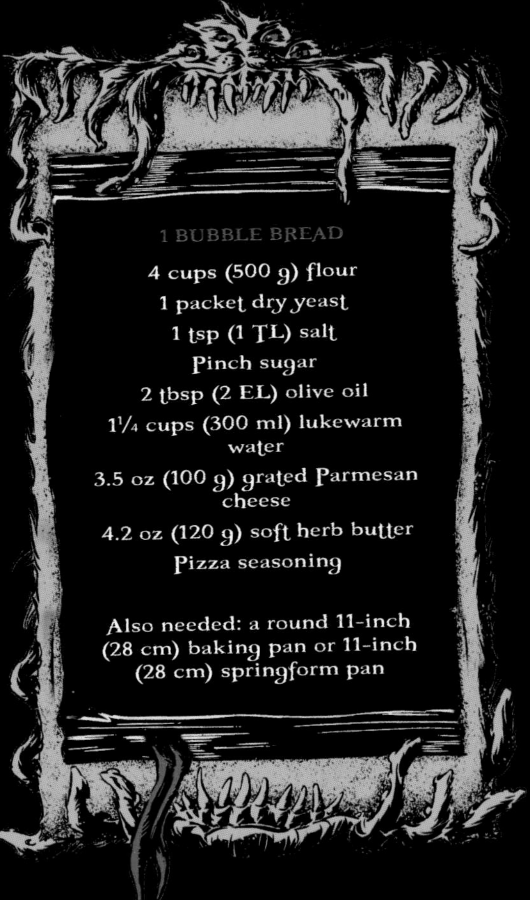

1 BUBBLE BREAD
4 cups (500 g) flour
1 packet dry yeast
1 tsp (1 TL) salt
Pinch sugar
2 tbsp (2 EL) olive oil
1¼ cups (300 ml) lukewarm water
3.5 oz (100 g) grated Parmesan cheese
4.2 oz (120 g) soft herb butter
Pizza seasoning
Also needed: a round 11-inch (28 cm) baking pan or 11-inch (28 cm) springform pan

1. Mix the flour and dry yeast in a mixing bowl. Add the salt, sugar, and oil. Add the water. Knead everything thoroughly with your hands for at least 10 minutes. Then loosely cover with a dish towel and leave to rise in a warm place for at least 50 minutes.
2. When the dough has risen, add half of the grated cheese and again knead thoroughly. Cut out ½ ounce (15 g) of dough at a time, shape into balls, and place together side by side on the baking sheet or in the springform pan to form a round loaf. Cover and let rise for 15 minutes.
3. Meanwhile, brush a round baking pan (11 inches/28 cm across) generously with 1.8 ounces (50 g) of the herb butter. Melt the remaining herb butter in a small bowl in the microwave, add the pizza seasoning if you like, and mix together.
4. Preheat the oven to 355°F (180°C).
5. Using a pastry brush, brush the bubble bread generously with the spiced butter. Bake in the oven for 15 minutes. Then sprinkle the rest of the Parmesan cheese on top and bake for another 5 to 10 minutes until golden brown. Allow to cool for a few minutes before serving.
6. Serve, if desired, with devil sauce, guacamole, and tzatziki (see Hell Served Three Ways, page 89).

Sneaky Sandwich

This is a real killer! This sandwich version of a giant snake will take out any hunger pangs in no time at all.

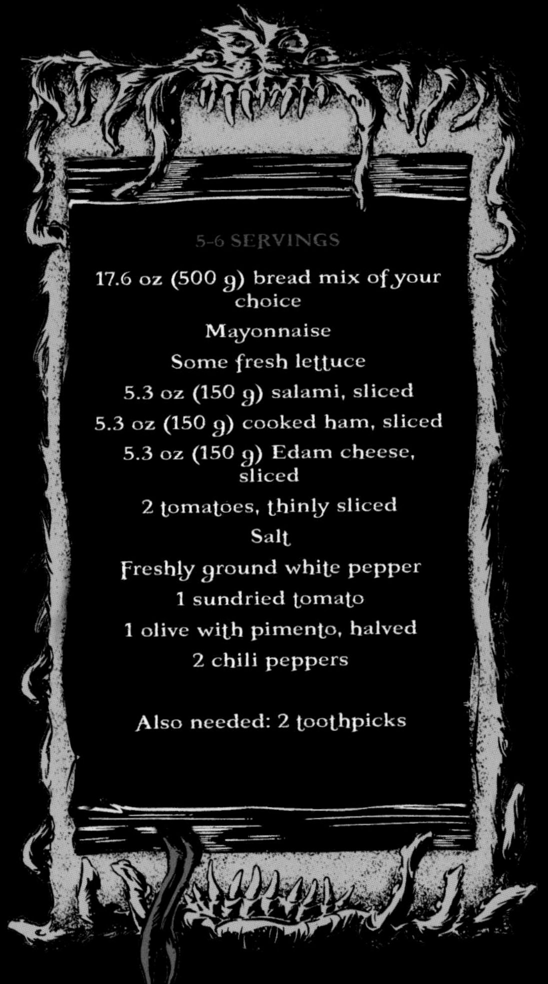

5–6 SERVINGS

17.6 oz (500 g) bread mix of your choice
Mayonnaise
Some fresh lettuce
5.3 oz (150 g) salami, sliced
5.3 oz (150 g) cooked ham, sliced
5.3 oz (150 g) Edam cheese, sliced
2 tomatoes, thinly sliced
Salt
Freshly ground white pepper
1 sundried tomato
1 olive with pimento, halved
2 chili peppers

Also needed: 2 toothpicks

1. Prepare the bread dough according to package instructions. On a lightly floured surface, form an oblong loaf with your hands, flatten slightly and shape into a rough S-shape, resembling a serpentine slithering snake. Lightly score the top diagonally with a knife at regular intervals. Place carefully on a baking sheet lined with parchment paper and bake in the preheated oven according to the instructions (usually about 20–30 minutes). Remove from the oven and let cool on the baking sheet for 20 minutes.
2. As soon as the bread snake has cooled, cut it completely lengthwise so that there's a bottom and top half. Spread some mayonnaise on the underside, cover with fresh lettuce, and generously add the salami, boiled ham, cheese, and tomato slices. Season with salt and pepper to taste. Add some more mayonnaise and close the sandwich by placing the other bread half on top. Lightly press down.
3. Cut a long, sundried tomato on one side to resemble a snake's forked tongue, and place in the mouth of the sandwich snake.
4. Carefully poke two eye sockets into the snake's head with a small, sharp knife. Insert a halved olive with pimento into each so that it resembles two eyes.
5. Push a toothpick halfway into each chili pepper and attach it to the upper jaw of the sandwich snake (see picture). Serve promptly.

Crazy-Eyed Skewers

Fierce paranoia and wide, conspicuous, magically enhanced fake eyeballs are the inspiration behind these stunning skewers.

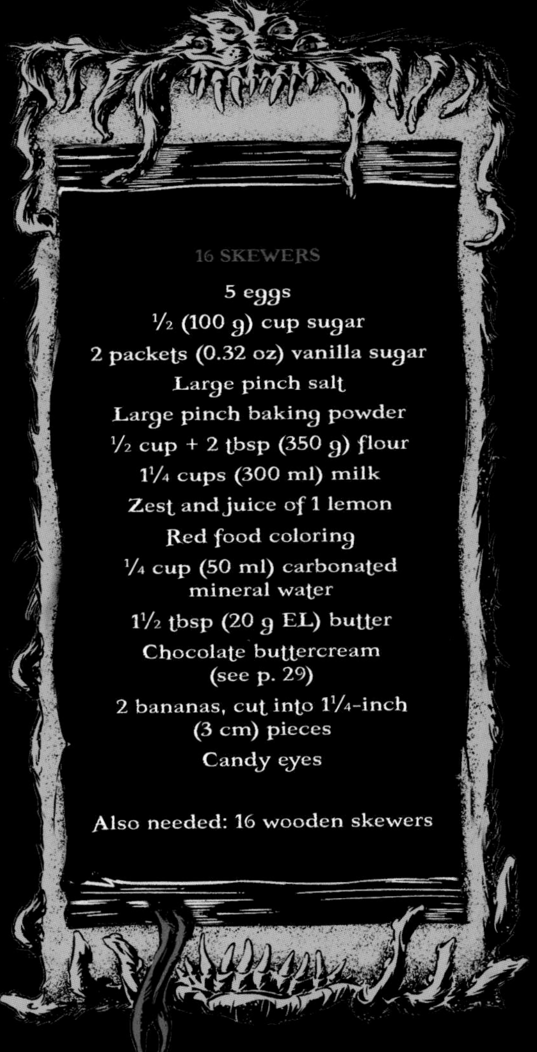

16 SKEWERS

5 eggs

½ (100 g) cup sugar

2 packets (0.32 oz) vanilla sugar

Large pinch salt

Large pinch baking powder

½ cup + 2 tbsp (350 g) flour

1¼ cups (300 ml) milk

Zest and juice of 1 lemon

Red food coloring

¼ cup (50 ml) carbonated mineral water

1½ tbsp (20 g EL) butter

Chocolate buttercream (see p. 29)

2 bananas, cut into 1¼-inch (3 cm) pieces

Candy eyes

Also needed: 16 wooden skewers

1. Beat the eggs, sugar, and vanilla sugar in a bowl with a hand mixer until fluffy. Stir in the salt, baking powder, flour, milk, lemon juice, and lemon zest. Mix everything together until the batter (which should be as smooth and liquid as possible) starts to develop slight bubbles. Then put the dough in the refrigerator for 30 minutes.
2. Meanwhile, mix some red food coloring with water.
3. After the dough has finished resting, add a dash of mineral water to it. Mix everything thoroughly again.
4. Melt the butter in a frying pan. Then remove from the heat and swivel so that the butter is evenly distributed across the hot pan.
5. Pour a ladleful of batter into the pan for each pancake and swivel briefly so that the bottom of the pan is completely covered with batter. Now cook the pancakes over medium heat. Once the top has set and the pancake can be easily lifted with a spatula, it's firm enough to flip and cook the other side until golden brown. Put the finished pancake on a flat plate and follow the above process for the rest of the batter.
6. Spread chocolate buttercream all over the pancake and place a peeled banana in the middle. Now carefully roll the pancake around the banana. Using a sharp knife, cut the pancake with the banana into pieces about 1¼ inches (3 cm) wide and cut those into two pieces each. Stick on a wooden skewer so that it looks like a pair of eyes.
7. Gently press a candy eye into each banana slice to form the eyes. Now use a fine brush or a toothpick with the food coloring to apply the red veins to the eyes as the finishing touch.

GR
FFINDOR

There are things that simply belong at a proper Halloween party: Spoiled Fish (p Pastries and Moldy Cheese (p. 51), and Magic Bubble Bread (p. 83)—and of course, all these delicacies!

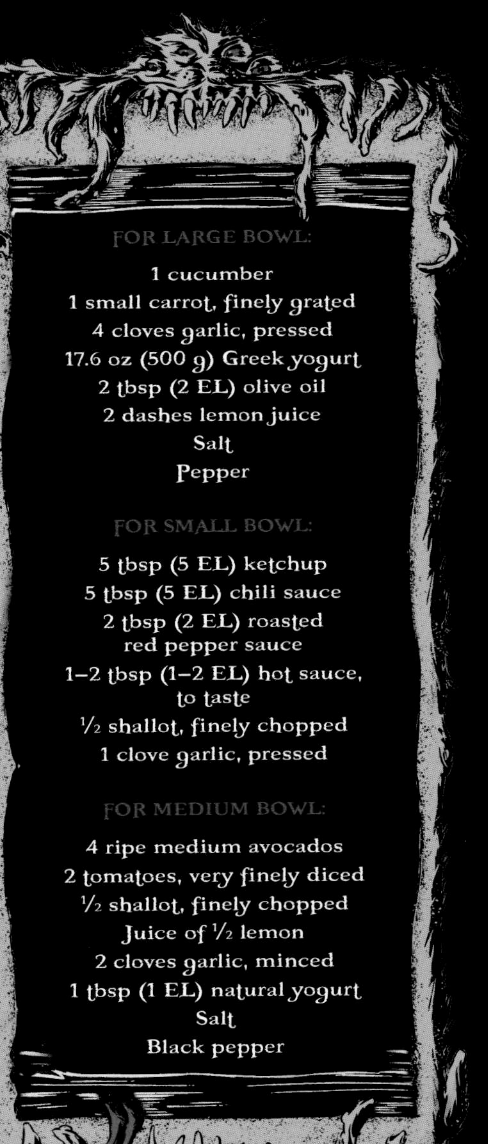

FOR LARGE BOWL:
1 cucumber
1 small carrot, finely grated
4 cloves garlic, pressed
17.6 oz (500 g) Greek yogurt
2 tbsp (2 EL) olive oil
2 dashes lemon juice
Salt
Pepper
FOR SMALL BOWL:
5 tbsp (5 EL) ketchup
5 tbsp (5 EL) chili sauce
2 tbsp (2 EL) roasted red pepper sauce
1–2 tbsp (1–2 EL) hot sauce, to taste
½ shallot, finely chopped
1 clove garlic, pressed
FOR MEDIUM BOWL:
4 ripe medium avocados
2 tomatoes, very finely diced
½ shallot, finely chopped
Juice of ½ lemon
2 cloves garlic, minced
1 tbsp (1 EL) natural yogurt
Salt
Black pepper

Tzatzik

1. Wash the cucumber, peel, and h the seeds. Grate the cucumber, generously. After 30 minutes, d save the cucumber water. Place kitchen towel and squeeze out t Pour the cucumber pulp into a cucumber water aside.
2. Place the carrot and garlic clove with the yogurt, cucumber pulp Stir thoroughly. Season with ol as well as generously with salt a with plastic wrap and let sit in least 6 hours, preferably overni again before serving. Enjoy slig

Devil Sa

1. In a small bowl, add the ketchu red pepper sauce, and optional on how hot you want the dip t and garlic and stir well. Cover and chill in the refrigerator for thoroughly again before serving

Guacam

1. Carefully halve the avocados ar the inside out of the skin with with a fork in a bowl. Add the lemon juice, garlic, and yogurt you like it finer, you should use Season with salt and pepper. St before serving! Best enjoyed sli

Magic Apples

Every child knows that magical apples should be avoided, as the consequences for those who taste them are usually rather unpleasant. Luckily, this particular kind is totally different: All that awaits you after eating these magic apples is happiness. That, and maybe a modest sugar rush . . .

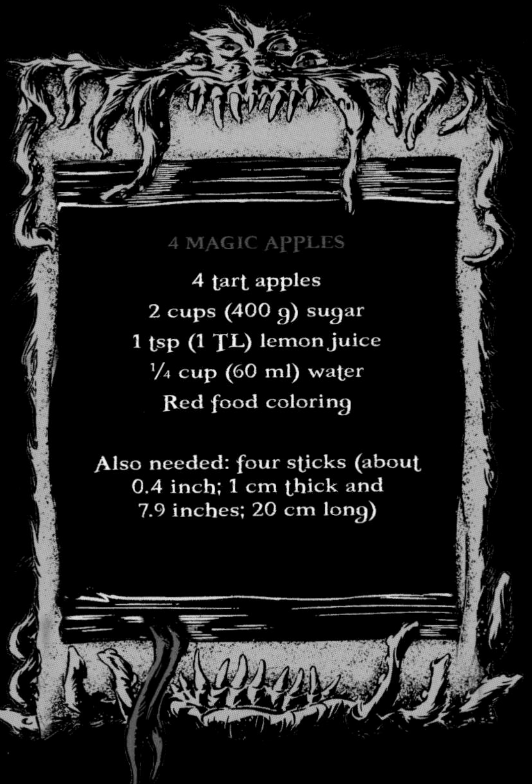

4 MAGIC APPLES
4 tart apples
2 cups (400 g) sugar
1 tsp (1 TL) lemon juice
¼ cup (60 ml) water
Red food coloring
Also needed: four sticks (about 0.4 inch; 1 cm thick and 7.9 inches; 20 cm long)

1. Line a baking sheet with parchment paper.
2. Wash and dry the apples thoroughly. Remove the stems and insert a stick into each apple so that the apple is firmly embedded on it.
3. In a medium saucepan, heat the sugar, lemon juice, and water over medium-high heat, stirring constantly. Stir until the sugar has completely dissolved. Stir in enough of the food coloring to achieve the desired shade of red. Then let the mixture simmer, stirring constantly, until it starts to caramelize.
4. Take the pot off the stove, place it on a heat-resistant surface, and dip the apples one by one upside down into the viscous mixture. Caution: Very hot! Slowly twist and turn the apple until it is coated all over with the red candy coating.
5. Let the excess candy coating drip off. Place the apples on the prepared baking sheet to dry, touching the parchment paper as little as possible. It is best if enjoyed on the same day, but within three days of preparation at most.

Chopped Toffees

Your friends' tongues won't swell and grow up to a meter long when they chomp on this toffee, but it's still magical—magically delicious!

5-6 SERVINGS

25 crackers (such as Ritz)
2 sticks (220 g) butter
1 cup (200 g) sugar
12.3 oz (350 g) dark chocolate for coating, coarsely chopped
To decorate: small pretzels, brittle, chopped pecans, etc.

1. Line a small tray with parchment paper and preheat the oven to 340°F (170°C).
2. Spread the crackers smoothly across the sheet in an even layer.
3. Place the butter and sugar in a small saucepan and bring to a slow boil over medium-high heat, stirring regularly. simmering for 2 minutes.
4. Pour the butter-sugar mixture evenly over the crackers, spread evenly with a kitchen spatula and place in the preheated oven for about 10 minutes. Then take it out and let cool for a few minutes.
5. Meanwhile, melt the dark chocolate in a small bowl over a bain-marie or using a double boiler. Be careful not to let the bottom of the bowl touch the water. Then pour the melted chocolate evenly over the cooled toffee crackers and gently smooth out with the spatula. Now decorate to your heart's content, with small pretzels, brittle, and chopped pecans. Then let harden.
6. Cut the tongue toffees into pieces as desired on a cutting board using a large, sharp knife and store in an airtight container.

Scraps of Crunchy Skin

No question about it, the best part of fried chicken is the skin, nice and crispy and flavorful! Unfortunately, apart from the skin, chickens have all sorts of other things attached to them, like the entire rest of the bird. In order to serve up a decent amount of this delicious snack, you either need a lot of dead poultry and a lot of time—or save yourself the drudgery of skinning one chicken after another and simply order the skin from your trusted butcher without the rest of the bird's annoying trappings!

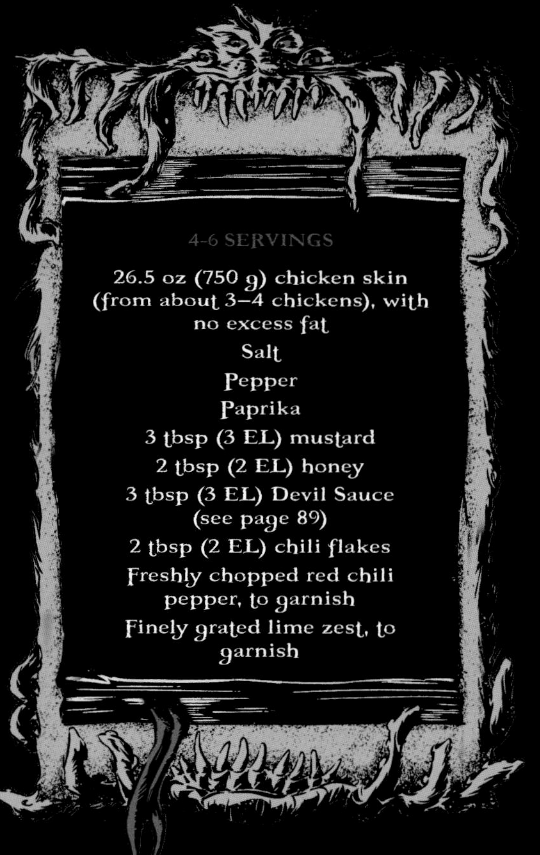

4–6 SERVINGS

26.5 oz (750 g) chicken skin (from about 3–4 chickens), with no excess fat
Salt
Pepper
Paprika
3 tbsp (3 EL) mustard
2 tbsp (2 EL) honey
3 tbsp (3 EL) Devil Sauce (see page 89)
2 tbsp (2 EL) chili flakes
Freshly chopped red chili pepper, to garnish
Finely grated lime zest, to garnish

1. Preheat the oven to 355°F (180°C), and line a baking sheet with parchment paper.
2. Cut the chicken skin into pieces 3.9 inches/10 cm in diameter (since they will shrink noticeably during cooking). Season both sides lightly with salt, pepper, and paprika. Place the chicken skin pieces on the baking sheet with a little space between them. Place another sheet of parchment paper on top, and then a second baking sheet or other weight to hold it down. This keeps the chips nice and flat. Cook in the oven for about 20 minutes.
3. Meanwhile, in a small bowl, stir together the mustard, honey, and Devil Sauce with the chili flakes. When finished cooking, brush the tops of the chicken skin pieces generously with the mixture. Turn the scraps of skin after 10 minutes and brush the top again with the hot sauce. Cook for another 10 minutes until the chicken chips are nice and crispy and golden brown.
4. Place the chicken chips on a plate lined with paper towels to drain. Allow to cool slightly. Sprinkle sparingly with the freshly grated lemon zest just before serving. Serve with Devil's Sauce as a dip, if you like.

It makes the most sense to combine this recipe with a chicken fricassee or a similar poultry dish to get the necessary chicken skin without much effort. Alternatively, you can easily order chicken skin online.

Meaty Tarantula Eyes

As if to compensate for how hard spider eyes are to come by, once you have them, they have countless uses. For example, you can use them to make magical potions and ointments, to make punches—or you can simply eat them raw, as a snack. Now that lets eye candy take on a whole new meaning!

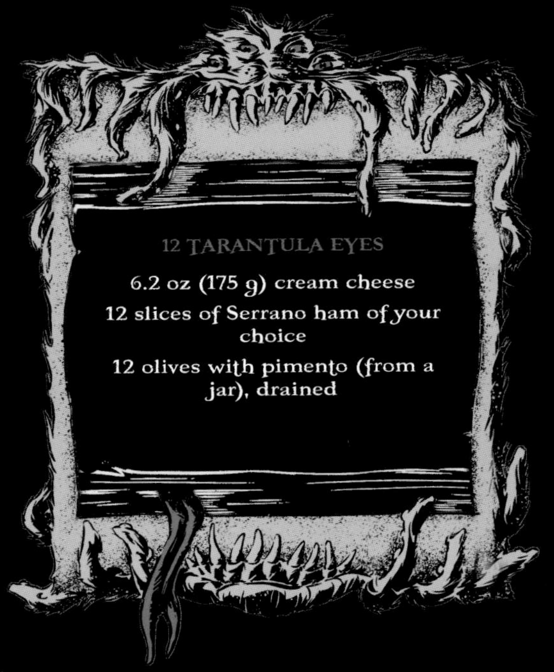

12 TARANTULA EYES

6.2 oz (175 g) cream cheese

12 slices of Serrano ham of your choice

12 olives with pimento (from a jar), drained

1. Drain the cream cheese using a sieve. Gently squeeze with your hands to wring out as much of the remaining liquid as possible.
2. Form the cream cheese into eyeball-sized balls. Push in an olive with the pimento "iris" so that about ⅓ of the olive sticks out, and gently press on the cream cheese.
3. Wrap a slice of ham around each ball to resemble an eyeball. Arrange on a large serving plate, spaced slightly apart. Store loosely covered with plastic wrap in the refrigerator until just before serving.

Astral Droppings

Every living being has to feed on something, and whatever is indigestible and left over is excreted. This applies to all life. That's how nature works. These specific excretions are known to feed on negative emotions. However, these droppings are surprisingly delicious. Just don't think about where they come from . . .

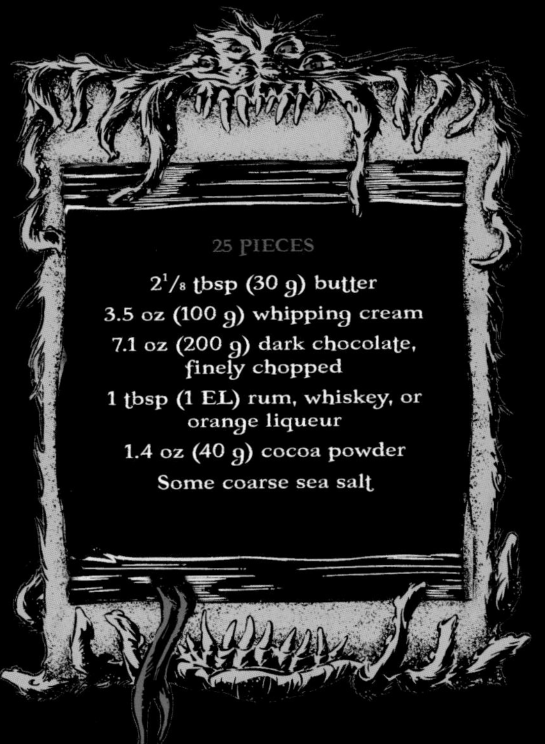

25 PIECES

2 1/8 tbsp (30 g) butter
3.5 oz (100 g) whipping cream
7.1 oz (200 g) dark chocolate, finely chopped
1 tbsp (1 EL) rum, whiskey, or orange liqueur
1.4 oz (40 g) cocoa powder
Some coarse sea salt

1. Cut the butter into small pieces. Bring the cream to a boil in a small saucepan over low heat, remove from the heat, and add the chopped chocolate and butter. Wait a moment, then stir until everything is completely melted. Allow to cool again and stir in the alcohol. Place the mixture in the refrigerator for at least 3 to 4 hours, preferably overnight.
2. Use your hands to form small, bite-size balls (2 in/5 cm diameter) from the cooled mixture, roll them in cocoa powder, and sprinkle with coarse sea salt on all sides. Caution: the mass melts very quickly and sticks to your fingers. Work as quickly as possible, rinse your hands with cold water from time to time, and dry them well! The Astral Droppings can be stored in the refrigerator for several days.

You can also leave out the alcohol if you wish. Then the orbs are still delicious, but not quite as aromatic.

Magic Cauldron

Everyone has their favorite subjects in school as well as the ones they dislike. If you're training to be a wizard, a course in potions may or may not be a favorite of yours. Even if you're not a fan, it's hard to resist these delicious magic cauldrons for brewing potions!

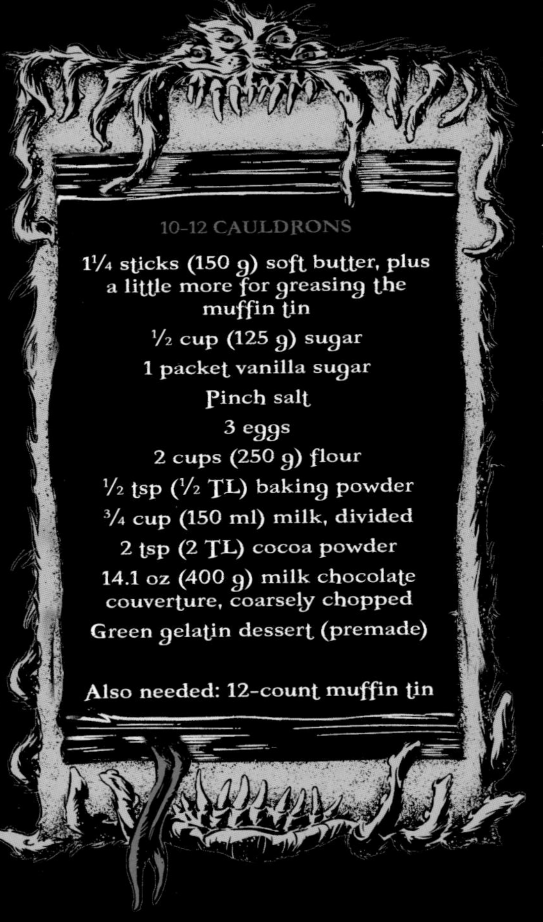

10-12 CAULDRONS
1¼ sticks (150 g) soft butter, plus a little more for greasing the muffin tin
½ cup (125 g) sugar
1 packet vanilla sugar
Pinch salt
3 eggs
2 cups (250 g) flour
½ tsp (½ TL) baking powder
¾ cup (150 ml) milk, divided
2 tsp (2 TL) cocoa powder
14.1 oz (400 g) milk chocolate couverture, coarsely chopped
Green gelatin dessert (premade)
Also needed: 12-count muffin tin

1. Preheat the oven to 355°F (180°C). Grease the muffin tin with some butter.
2. In a bowl, beat together the butter with the sugar, vanilla sugar, and salt using an electric hand mixer. Then work in the eggs one at a time.
3. In a separate bowl, mix the flour and baking powder together, adding each little by little; Add a little milk (½ cup/125 ml) in intervals. Work through everything thoroughly. Then pour ¾ of the dough into the prepared muffin tin.
4. Mix the rest of the batter with the remaining milk and cocoa powder. Divide the chocolate batter evenly over the light batter in the muffin cups. Mix the batter in the baking molds with a small dessert fork.
5. Bake the muffins in the oven for about 25 to 30 minutes. Then take the tin out and let cool completely in the tin.
6. When the muffins have cooled, carefully remove them from the tin and place them upside down on the work surface. (If necessary, level the underside with a sharp knife so that the cauldrons stand up better.) Then carefully cut out the cauldron opening with a small, sharp knife and a small spoon and hollow out the muffin about .4 to .8 inch (1 to 2 cm) deep. Make sure that the cauldron sides remain intact!
7. Melt the couverture over a bain-marie. Place a small portion of the couverture in a piping bag fitted with a very fine tip. Line a baking sheet with parchment paper and pipe the cauldrons' handles onto it using the piping bag. It is best to draw the desired shape with a pen on the parchment paper beforehand. Allow the chocolate to set.
8. Meanwhile, use a pastry brush to evenly coat the muffins all around with the remaining couverture. Feel free to add a bit more to make the whole thing more cauldron-like (see image). Put a handle on each cauldron; possibly adhere with some couverture. Store in the refrigerator until ready to serve.
9. Immediately before serving, take the gelatin out of the refrigerator, coarsely chop it, and carefully add some of it to the cauldron with a small spoon. Serve immediately.

Wolfsbane Potion

Full Moon Potion

If you happen to know any werewolves, serve this up the week before the full moon to help them keep control of their human minds during their transformations into terrifying monsters. Best to brew enough of this right away so that you are always on the safe side!

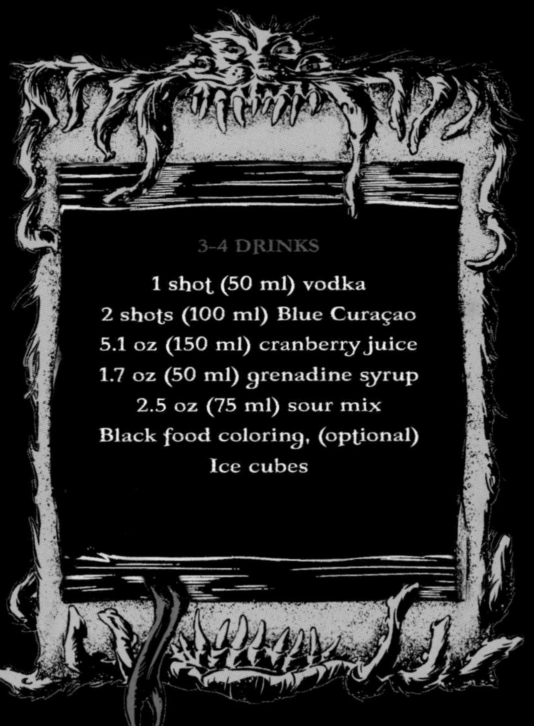

3–4 DRINKS

1 shot (50 ml) vodka
2 shots (100 ml) Blue Curaçao
5.1 oz (150 ml) cranberry juice
1.7 oz (50 ml) grenadine syrup
2.5 oz (75 ml) sour mix
Black food coloring, (optional)
Ice cubes

1. In a small pitcher, stir together the vodka, Blue Curaçao, cranberry juice, grenadine, and sour mix. If the coloring is not purple enough, add 1 or 2 drops of black food coloring and stir thoroughly.
2. Place a few ice cubes in each tumbler, then add the Full Moon Potion and serve immediately.

To brew a less-potent version of this potion, simply omit the vodka and use the nonalcoholic Blue Curacao instead of the alcoholic version!

Dragon Meatballs

Not all, but many dragons are pretty nasty creatures that transport unwary souls to the afterlife faster than desired. That said, dragons can also be very pleasing—yes, if properly seasoned and prepared, they are a real treat for the palate!

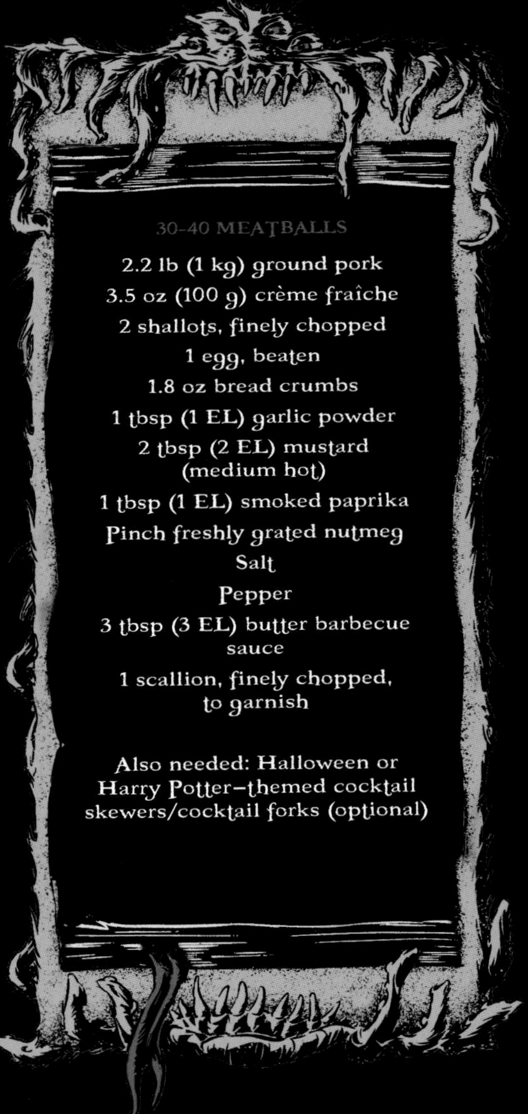

30–40 MEATBALLS

2.2 lb (1 kg) ground pork

3.5 oz (100 g) crème fraîche

2 shallots, finely chopped

1 egg, beaten

1.8 oz bread crumbs

1 tbsp (1 EL) garlic powder

2 tbsp (2 EL) mustard (medium hot)

1 tbsp (1 EL) smoked paprika

Pinch freshly grated nutmeg

Salt

Pepper

3 tbsp (3 EL) butter barbecue sauce

1 scallion, finely chopped, to garnish

Also needed: Halloween or Harry Potter–themed cocktail skewers/cocktail forks (optional)

1. In a mixing bowl, combine the ground pork, crème fraîche, shallots, egg, bread crumbs, garlic powder, mustard, paprika, and nutmeg, season with salt and pepper to taste, and work vigorously with your hands to mix well mix.
2. With slightly moistened hands, work the ground pork mixture to form bite-size balls.
3. Put the butter in the largest possible pan and melt over medium-high heat. Gradually, in several batches, sear the meatballs vigorously on all sides (5 minutes); turn several times. Place the fried meatballs on a paper-towel-lined plate to drain.
4. Arrange the fried meatballs on a large serving plate. Drizzle with barbecue sauce and sprinkle with some freshly chopped scallion. Stick a Halloween or Harry Potter skewer/cocktail fork into each dragon meatball, if you like, and serve as soon as possible to avoid drying out the balls.

Hearty Hate Mail

You may have heard that these magical envelopes will shrilly insist on being opened, only shutting up after showering the recipient with a veritable tirade. However, these hearty pieces of hate mail are quite different: it's safe to open them, and what's in store for you is guaranteed to be anything but nasty!

4 PIECES OF HEARTY HATE MAIL

2 (14-oz; 400-g) packages of frozen pizza dough

4–6 tbsp (4–6 EL) tomato sauce

Pizza seasoning

8 slices of cooked ham

4 slices of semihard cheese (such as Gouda)

1 egg, lightly beaten

¼ red pepper

4 black olives, pitted

Also needed: a classic square envelope (optional)

1. Take the frozen dough out of the refrigerator and let it thaw for 10 minutes. Spread it out on the work surface. Roll it out a little thinner toward the shorter sides so that the dough lengthens and you get a rough rectangle. Then halve this rectangle so that you get two pieces measuring 9½ × 9½ inches (24 cm × 24 cm) each. If you don't have enough dough for this size, simply adjust the dimensions accordingly so both halves are still even.
2. Preheat the oven to 390°F (200°C).
3. Place the squares on a baking sheet lined with parchment paper so that you have two diamonds in front of you; this makes it easier to fold the dough sheets like envelopes. If you have a suitable envelope on hand, place it flush against the diamonds. Use the back of a knife to mark the fold lines—this will make it easier to turn the corners later. But careful: don't cut through the dough!
4. Spread some tomato sauce in the inner square, sprinkle with pizza seasoning, then place the ham and cheese on top. Make sure that the edges and corners of the dough remain free.
5. Now carefully fold over the corners with a wide knife or an icing spatula. First the side corners, then the bottom and finally the top. Using a pastry brush, brush the edges with the beaten egg to help the whole thing stick together. Bake in the preheated oven for about 20 to 25 minutes.
6. Meanwhile, cut the peppers into mouth-shaped strips and the olives into eyelike wedges.
7. Once the envelopes are done baking, remove from the oven and attach the mouth and eyes using some beaten egg as adhesive. Serve immediately.

Pumpkin Pasties

These pasties are so good, they may be the food that fuels a new friendship for you this Halloween season!

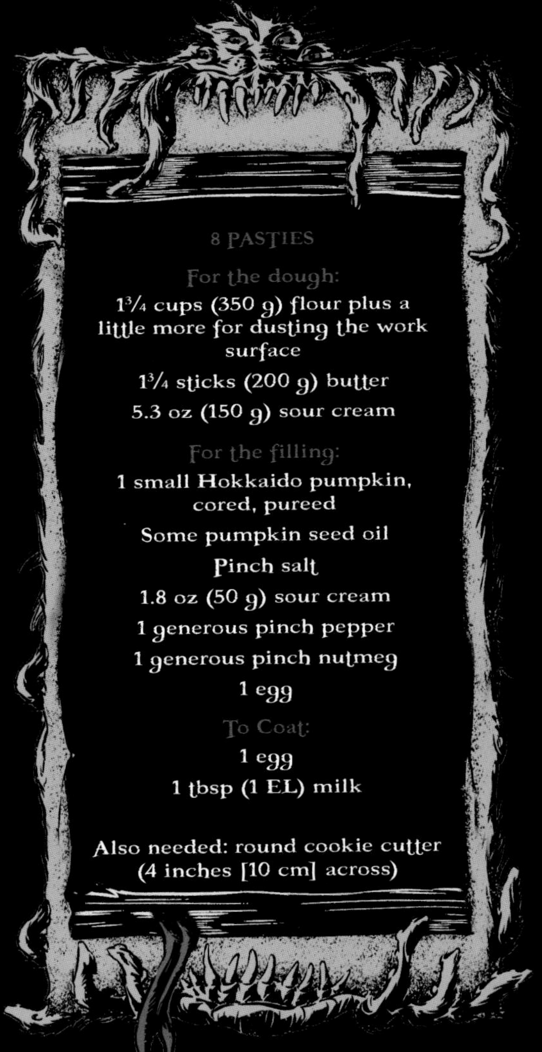

8 PASTIES

For the dough:

1¾ cups (350 g) flour plus a little more for dusting the work surface

1¾ sticks (200 g) butter

5.3 oz (150 g) sour cream

For the filling:

1 small Hokkaido pumpkin, cored, pureed

Some pumpkin seed oil

Pinch salt

1.8 oz (50 g) sour cream

1 generous pinch pepper

1 generous pinch nutmeg

1 egg

To Coat:

1 egg

1 tbsp (1 EL) milk

Also needed: round cookie cutter (4 inches [10 cm] across)

1. Knead the flour, butter, and sour cream in a bowl to form a smooth, supple dough. Wrap tightly in plastic wrap and place in the refrigerator for 1 or 2 hours.
2. Preheat the oven to 350°F (175°C). Line a baking sheet with parchment paper.
3. Roll out the dough thinly on a lightly floured surface and cut out eight circles with a cookie cutter. Place them slightly apart on the prepared baking sheet.
4. Cook the pumpkin flesh together with the pumpkin seed oil and a little salt in a sufficiently large saucepan over medium heat while stirring regularly, then puree as finely as possible in the saucepan using an immersion blender. Add the sour cream and season generously with pepper and nutmeg. Add the egg and mix everything together thoroughly. Remove from the stove and let cool a bit.
5. Place a tablespoon of pumpkin filling on each circle of dough on the baking sheet, fold the dough over once and press down the edges with your fingers or a fork. Use a knife to cut three small vertical slits in each pasty to allow air to escape while baking.
6. In a small bowl, whisk together an egg and a tablespoon of milk. Brush the pasties fully and place in the oven for about 20 minutes until golden brown; turn once halfway through. Then remove and let cool on the tray for about 5 to 10 minutes. Best served lukewarm.

Bouncy Fungi

If you have enough of the Swamp Juice (p. 13), you may actually see these little mushroom tops jumping up and down before your very eyes!

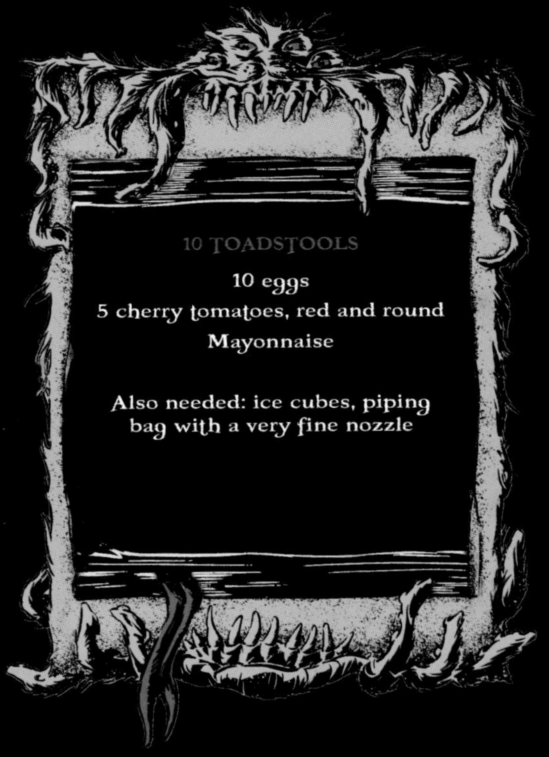

10 TOADSTOOLS

10 eggs
5 cherry tomatoes, red and round
Mayonnaise

Also needed: ice cubes, piping bag with a very fine nozzle

1. In a saucepan, hard-boil the eggs over medium-high heat (about 8 to 10 minutes).
2. Meanwhile, prepare an ice bath. To do so, place cold water and a few ice cubes in a medium bowl.
3. Using a ladle, take the hard-boiled eggs and stick them in the ice bath for a few seconds.
4. Halve the tomatoes, then cut out the stem and base. Carefully remove the seeds and a little of the flesh with a teaspoon. Make sure the skin remains intact! Then pat the tomato halves dry with paper towels.
5. Peel the eggs carefully and cut off a small piece on the underside with a sharp knife so that the eggs can stand more easily. Arrange on a serving plate, spaced slightly apart. Place a halved tomato on top of each egg to cap it.
6. Put the mayonnaise in a piping bag with a very fine nozzle and pipe small white dots onto the red caps at regular distances apart.

Tripe

There are things that you only really appreciate if you are into gourmet, come from Scotland—or have long since stuck a fork in it.

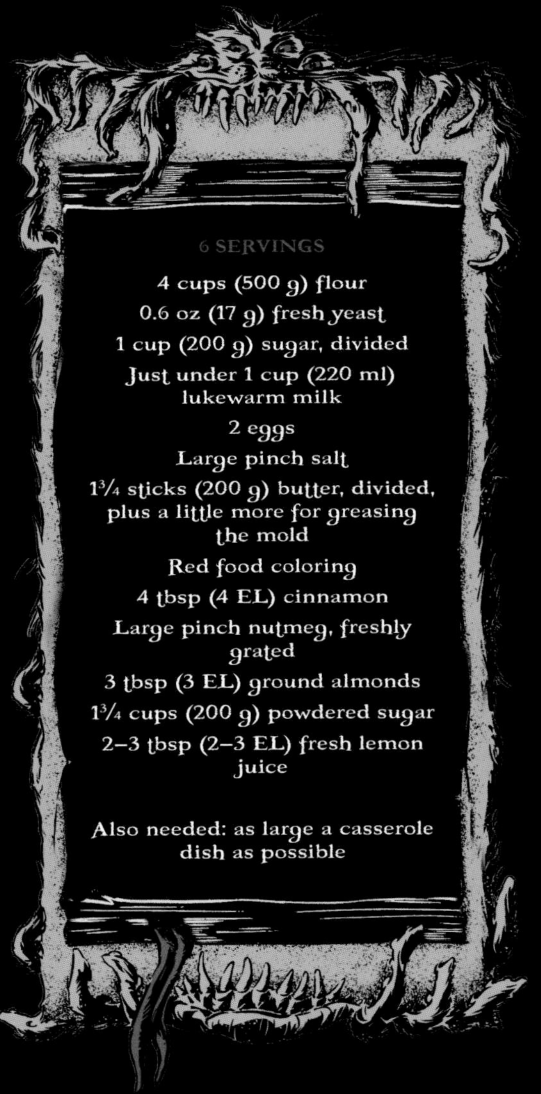

6 SERVINGS

4 cups (500 g) flour
0.6 oz (17 g) fresh yeast
1 cup (200 g) sugar, divided
Just under 1 cup (220 ml) lukewarm milk
2 eggs
Large pinch salt
1¾ sticks (200 g) butter, divided, plus a little more for greasing the mold
Red food coloring
4 tbsp (4 EL) cinnamon
Large pinch nutmeg, freshly grated
3 tbsp (3 EL) ground almonds
1¾ cups (200 g) powdered sugar
2–3 tbsp (2–3 EL) fresh lemon juice

Also needed: as large a casserole dish as possible

1. Place the flour in a large bowl and make an indent in the center. Crumble in the yeast and add ½ cup (100 g) of sugar and the milk. Mix everything briefly. Then gradually add the eggs, the salt, just under ¾ stick (80 g) of the butter, and three drops of red food coloring. Knead thoroughly to form a smooth, pliable dough. Cover the bowl with plastic wrap or a damp dish towel and leave to rise in a warm place for an hour.
2. In the meantime, prepare the filling. To do this, melt the remaining butter in a small saucepan, then add the cinnamon, remaining sugar, nutmeg, and ground almonds and mix everything together.
3. Once the dough has risen, form the guts. To do this, on a lightly floured work surface, shape the dough with your hands into uneven, sausage-thick strands. Butter a casserole dish that is as large as possible and place the intestines in it so that it looks appropriately disgusting. Spread the cinnamon mixture evenly over the dough strands with a spoon. Cover with plastic wrap or with a damp dish towel and let it rise again for about 15 minutes.
4. In the meantime, preheat the oven to 355°F (180°C).
5. Bake the "guts" after they've risen in the oven for about 30 minutes.
6. Meanwhile prepare the frosting. In a small bowl, mix together the powdered sugar, lemon juice, and 3 to 5 drops of red food coloring (depending on how gory you want it to be) until you get a smooth, viscous mass.
7. Take the guts out of the oven, let them cool in the pan for a few minutes, then spread the blood frosting evenly over them. Allow to cool again for a few minutes before serving.

Ash Ice Cream

Certain things simply naturally belong together. What, you haven't heard of this delicious combination of flavors yet? Well, then it's high time to change that!

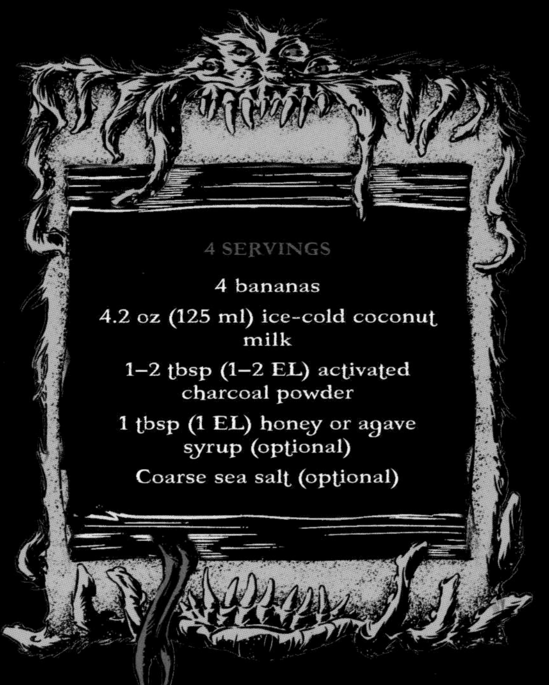

4 SERVINGS

4 bananas

4.2 oz (125 ml) ice-cold coconut milk

1–2 tbsp (1–2 EL) activated charcoal powder

1 tbsp (1 EL) honey or agave syrup (optional)

Coarse sea salt (optional)

1. Peel the bananas, cut them into small pieces, and place in the freezer for 3 or 4 hours or until the banana pieces are completely frozen.
2. Place the frozen banana pieces in a food processor or blender with the ice-cold coconut milk, the activated charcoal powder, and (if using) the honey or agave syrup and blend until you have a smooth ice cream base.
3. Pour the ice cream mixture into a flat mold and freeze for at least 2 hours.
4. Serve sprinkled with a little coarse sea salt, if you like.

Punch Bowl o' Shrunken Heads

Yet another shrunken head recipe, this time for a hearty party punch. These shriveled little things might not look like much, but they're certainly versatile!

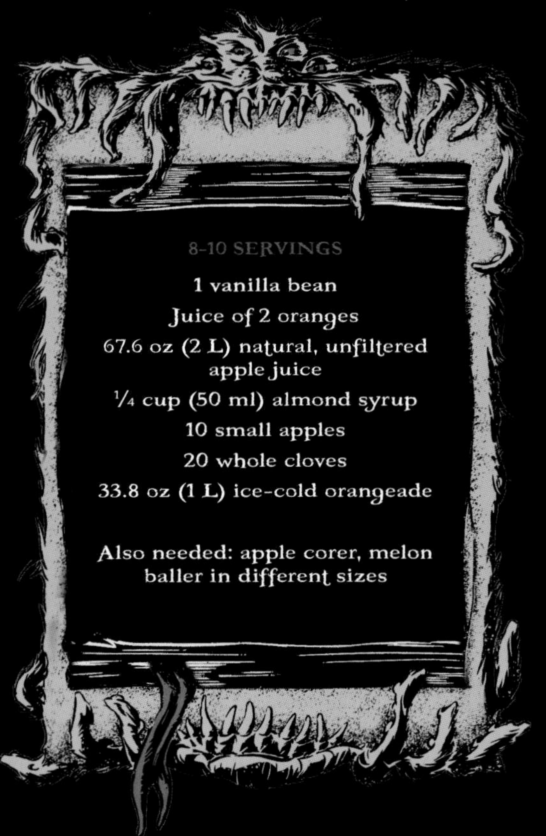

8–10 SERVINGS

1 vanilla bean

Juice of 2 oranges

67.6 oz (2 L) natural, unfiltered apple juice

¼ cup (50 ml) almond syrup

10 small apples

20 whole cloves

33.8 oz (1 L) ice-cold orangeade

Also needed: apple corer, melon baller in different sizes

1. Scrape out the vanilla pod and juice the oranges. Put the vanilla pulp and the orange juice together with the apple juice and the almond syrup in a sufficiently large saucepan and briefly bring to boil over medium heat, stirring regularly. Allow to cool and chill in the refrigerator for about 1 to 2 hours.
2. Meanwhile, preheat the oven to 300°F (150°C). Line a baking sheet with parchment paper.
3. Peel the apples carefully and remove the core with an apple corer. Pat the apples dry with a paper towel. Using a small, sharp kitchen knife, a melon baller, and cookie cutters, cut scary faces into the fruit's flesh. Insert a whole clove, stem-first, into each eye socket.
4. Place the apples faceup on the prepared baking sheet. Bake in the preheated oven for about 15 minutes until the shrunken heads are slightly browned and shriveled. Remove and let cool for a few minutes.
5. Pour the cooled vanilla apple juice into the punch bowl. Pour in the orangeade, stir well, and carefully add the shrunken heads. Serve immediately.

Licorice Slugs

These slick slugs are made of licorice and will snap at anyone who isn't careful enough. As for these special slugs, while they're a lot less harmless than those found any magical world, they're no less delicious!

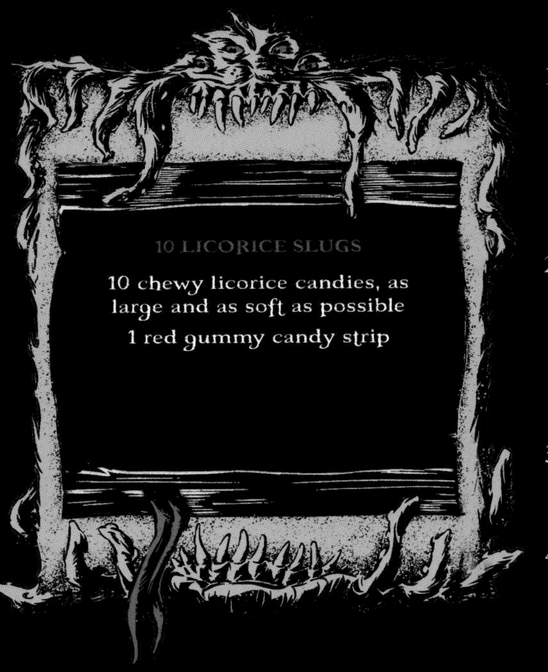

10 LICORICE SLUGS

10 chewy licorice candies, as large and as soft as possible
1 red gummy candy strip

1. Allow the chewy licorice candies to soften in a warm place for about 1 to 2 hours before handling so that they can be kneaded more easily. If that is not enough, warm each individually, if necessary, with your hands, using your own body heat. And if that's not enough, put it in the oven at the lowest heat.
2. Once the chewy candies are soft and easy to shape, form them into a ball. Then, with the palm of your hand, gently work into a cylinder or worm, with a thick, compact head that becomes noticeably narrower toward the tail end (see picture). Adjust the whole thing with your fingers.
3. Using a small, sharp knife, score parallel grooves at regular intervals in the back of the slug. Form a mouth with a toothpick and poke two holes for the eyes.
4. Cut the gummy fruit strip into pieces ⅕ inch (5 mm) long. Insert these pieces into the eye holes. Carefully heat with a lighter flame and round off a bit with your fingertips so that the eyes don't look so stubby. Store the licorice snaps in an airtight container.

For those who don't like licorice, you can easily make these slugs using soft toffee bonbons. The preparation process is exactly the same.

Caretaker's Cucumber Sandwich

A tame treat for your Halloween shindig, perhaps, but a wonderful way to pass the time.

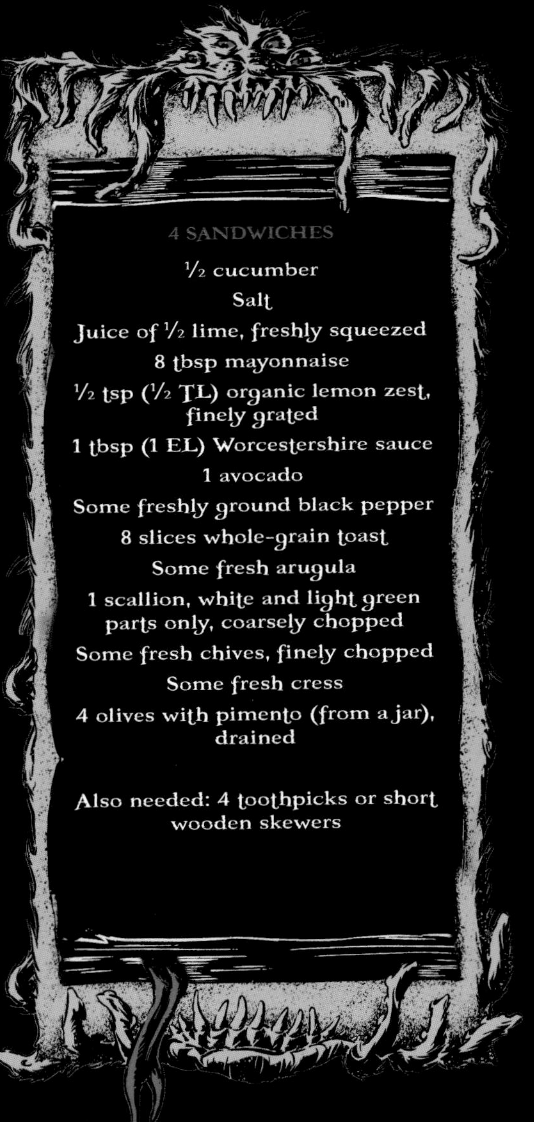

4 SANDWICHES

½ cucumber
Salt
Juice of ½ lime, freshly squeezed
8 tbsp mayonnaise
½ tsp (½ TL) organic lemon zest, finely grated
1 tbsp (1 EL) Worcestershire sauce
1 avocado
Some freshly ground black pepper
8 slices whole-grain toast
Some fresh arugula
1 scallion, white and light green parts only, coarsely chopped
Some fresh chives, finely chopped
Some fresh cress
4 olives with pimento (from a jar), drained

Also needed: 4 toothpicks or short wooden skewers

1. Peel the cucumber and cut in half lengthwise. Scoop out the seeds with a spoon and discard. Then slice the cucumber lengthwise into strips as thin as possible, place in a colander, generously salt, and drizzle with lime juice. Mix gently with your hands. Let sit for 15 minutes.
2. Meanwhile, in a small bowl, gently mix together the mayonnaise, lemon zest, and Worcestershire sauce until creamy.
3. Carefully halve the avocado. Remove the skin and the pit. Cut the fruit's flesh into fine slices. Sprinkle sparingly with some freshly ground black pepper.
4. Place four of the toast slices on the work surface and spread some of the spiced mayonnaise on them. Then layer the cucumber slices, arugula, and avocado slices on top as you like. Sprinkle with the scallion, the freshly chopped chives, and some cress. Finish with a layer of spiced mayonnaise and top each sandwich with another slice of toast. Press down carefully.
5. Stick a toothpick through the sandwich so that it holds it together and the toothpick tip sticks out a little at the top. Stick stuffed olive on top of the toothpick.

If you've already made the Demon Fingers (p. 11) and happen to have some of these nasty magical creatures' leftover digits, here's the ideal recipe for using those up: How about a delicious Demon Dog to celebrate the spookiest night of the year?

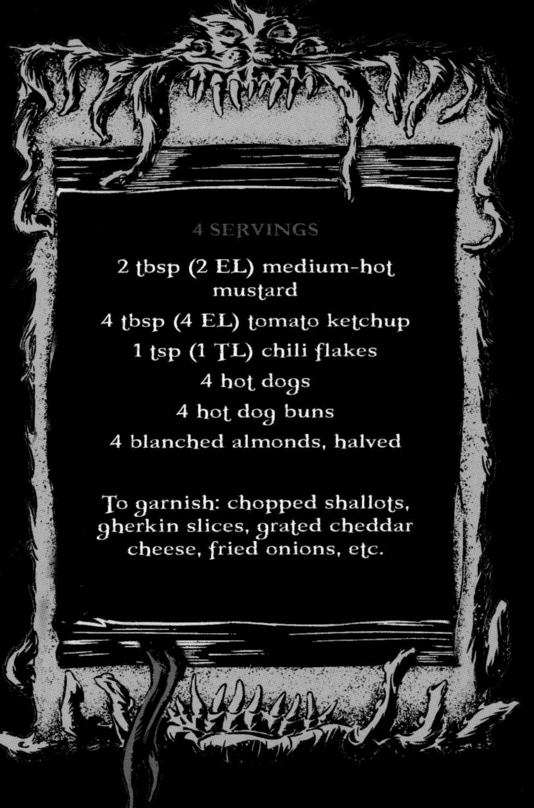

4 SERVINGS

2 tbsp (2 EL) medium-hot mustard

4 tbsp (4 EL) tomato ketchup

1 tsp (1 TL) chili flakes

4 hot dogs

4 hot dog buns

4 blanched almonds, halved

To garnish: chopped shallots, gherkin slices, grated cheddar cheese, fried onions, etc.

1. In a small bowl, stir together the mustard, ketchup, and chili flakes.
2. Heat enough water in a large saucepan. Use a knife to cut some of the skin and sausage meat from one end of each sausage, so as to resemble the position and size of a fingernail. Then place the sausages in the warm water and let soak for 5 minutes. Attention: the water must not boil, otherwise the sausages will burst!
3. Meanwhile, prepare the hot dog buns according to package directions. Carefully cut the warm buns lengthwise (but not all the way through!), and generously spread ketchup on the bottom half. Place a sausage on top with the nail bed facing up. Press a blanched almond onto the prepared area as a fingernail and use a small, sharp knife to cut three parallel grooves into the sausage as joint folds (see picture).
4. Serve in separate bowls with your favorite hot dog ingredients, such as fried onions, gherkins, or grated cheese.

Black Pudding

In England, Scotland, and Ireland, black pudding is often served with a hearty breakfast, but is sometimes also served as a starter. If featured at a Halloween party in the United States, the host may get a few looks—but it's the perfect night to try something new!

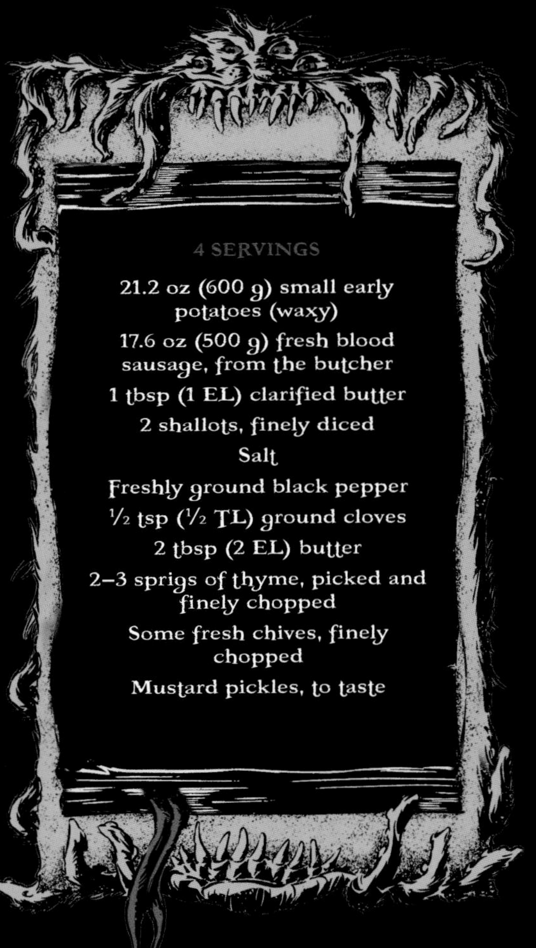

4 SERVINGS

21.2 oz (600 g) small early potatoes (waxy)

17.6 oz (500 g) fresh blood sausage, from the butcher

1 tbsp (1 EL) clarified butter

2 shallots, finely diced

Salt

Freshly ground black pepper

½ tsp (½ TL) ground cloves

2 tbsp (2 EL) butter

2–3 sprigs of thyme, picked and finely chopped

Some fresh chives, finely chopped

Mustard pickles, to taste

1. Wash and peel the potatoes and parboil them in a large pot of heavily salted water for about 15 to 20 minutes over medium heat. Drain and set aside for now.
2. Preheat the oven to 250°F (120°C).
3. Peel the blood sausage and cut into slices ¾ inch to 1 inch (2 to 3 cm) thick. Melt the clarified butter in a large pan and sweat the shallots in it until translucent.
4. Add the sausage slices and sear on both sides over medium heat (2 minutes each); turn as seldom as possible so that the sausage does not fall apart. Season generously with salt, freshly ground black pepper, and a tiny bit of ground cloves. Remove from the pan, place on a plate, cover loosely with aluminum foil and keep warm in the preheated oven until ready to serve.
5. Put the butter in the pan, increase the heat to high, and sauté the precooked potatoes with the thyme until golden brown on all sides. Season generously with salt and pepper, sprinkle with fresh chives, and serve with the sausage slices and mustard pickles.

Whole Salted Herring

These fish are generally served whole, including the head and tail. This will freak out a few guests, for sure!

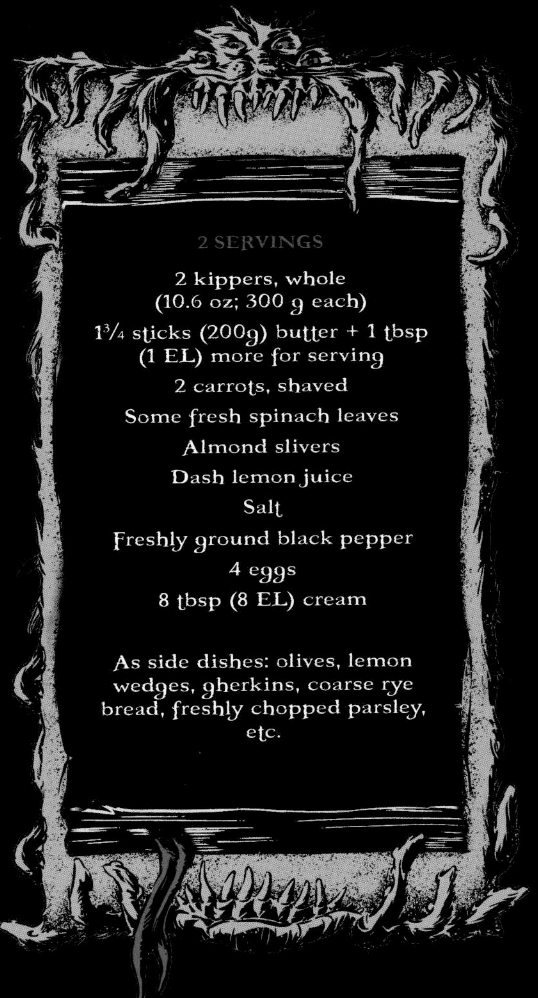

2 SERVINGS

2 kippers, whole (10.6 oz; 300 g each)

1¾ sticks (200g) butter + 1 tbsp (1 EL) more for serving

2 carrots, shaved

Some fresh spinach leaves

Almond slivers

Dash lemon juice

Salt

Freshly ground black pepper

4 eggs

8 tbsp (8 EL) cream

As side dishes: olives, lemon wedges, gherkins, coarse rye bread, freshly chopped parsley, etc.

Prepare the kippers:

1. Preheat the grill function of the oven to medium.
2. Add half the butter to the pan, melt over medium-high heat, stirring occasionally, and simmer until it turns brown and begins to smell nutty. Remove from the stove.
3. Lay the kippers side by side in a large casserole dish or on a baking sheet, pour over the butter, and place the fish directly under the oven grill. Cook for about 8 to 10 minutes; brush regularly with butter.
4. When the kippers are ready, arrange on a bed of carrot salad (see below) and serve with scrambled eggs (see below), 1 tablespoon butter, chopped parsley, pickles, lemon wedges, etc., if you wish.

Prepare the carrot salad:

5. In a bowl, mix the shaved carrot strips with some fresh spinach leaves, slivers of almonds, and a squeeze of lemon juice. Season generously with pepper and salt, mix well again, and leave to stand for at least 30 minutes before serving.

Prepare the scrambled eggs:

6. Crack the eggs into a bowl with a high rim, add the cream, season generously with salt and pepper and whisk until the whole thing is still relatively thick but nice and creamy.
7. Melt the other half of the butter in a nonstick pan over low heat. Add the beaten eggs and let stand. Carefully stir the bottom of the pan with a spatula from time to time so that the egg does not burn and becomes firmer throughout. When the scrambled eggs have reached the desired firmness, remove from the heat and serve immediately.

Acknowledgments

Just as good food and drink, per Gamp's Law of Elemental Transfiguration, cannot be conjured up out of thin air, no one—Muggle or Magical—produces a cookbook like this all by themselves. (It's quite possible that this is another Major Exception to Gamp's Law.) In reality, many talented people have worked wonders over months, even without magical powers, to ensure that this book, which is dear to my heart, is now in your hands.

They are: Jo Löffler & Holger "Holle" Wiest, my "Dinos," without whom nothing would be as it is; Roberts "Rob" Urlovskis, who uses a PC instead of a wand to cast his magic; Angelos Tsirigotis, my Swabian Greek (or Greek Swabian), for his terrific contributions to this book; Oskar "Ossi" Böhm & Annelies Haubold; the "K-Clan" of Tobi, Andrea, Finja & Lea; Katharina "The Only True Cat" Böhm; my "Brother from Another Mother" Thomas B. and his family, for many unforgettable moments in the past, present, and future; Ulrich "The Plague" Peste, for the same reasons; Dimitrie Harder, my "Partner in Crime" in all things cookbooks and the only person on earth who has ever called me a bully with impunity; Thomas Stamm and his wife Alexandra, for their appreciation and friendship; Karin Michelberger, Franz-Christoph Heel, and the lovely Hannah Kwella, for the many great projects; and last but not least, the rest of my family, who over and over give me the time, strength, and freedom to experience great adventures like this.

A special thank-you also goes out to my cousin and friend, Michél Kevin Hubel, who passed away completely unexpectedly and much too young at the age of only thirty-seven during the production of this book. Some might consider it disrespectful to dedicate a Halloween cookbook to a loved one, but anyone who knew Michél knows that the gesture would have been appreciated. I miss you, buddy. The thought of never again talking shop with you about films, computer games, and TV series is still incomprehensible to me. Keep an eye on us from up there, okay?

For everything that you readers like about this work, the thanks go to these wonderful people. On the other hand, you are welcome to have me don sackcloth and ashes for all the deficiencies in content, questionable formulations, incorrect quantities, and too much celery salt, preferably using the following social media channels: